RAISE YOUR
SOCIAL I.Q.

Also by Michael Levine

The Address Book
Guerrilla P.R.
Lessons at the Halfway Point
The Princess and the Package
Selling Goodness

RAISE YOUR
SOCIAL I.Q.

How to Do the Right Thing
in Any Situation

MICHAEL LEVINE

A Citadel Press Book
Published by Carol Publishing Group

Copyright © 1998 Michael Levine

A Citadel Press Book
Published by Carol Publishing Group
Citadel Press is a registered trademark of Carol Communications, Inc.

Editorial, sales and distribution, rights and permissions inquiries should be addressed to Carol Publishing Group, 120 Enterprise Avenue, Secaucus, N.J. 07094.

In Canada: Canadian Manda Group, One Atlantic Avenue, Suite 105, Toronto, Ontario M6K 3E7

Carol Publishing Group books may be purchased in bulk at special discounts for sales promotion, fund-raising, or educational purposes. Special editions can be created to specifications. For details, contact Special Sales Department, Carol Publishing Group, 120 Enterprise Avenue, Secaucus, N.J. 07094.

Manufactured in the United States of America

10   9   8   7   6   5   4   3   2   1

Library of Congress Cataloging-in-Publication Data

Levine, Michael, 1954–
      Raise your social I.Q. : how to do the right thing in any
   situation / Michael Levine.
         p.   cm.
      "A Citadel Press book."
      ISBN 0–8065–2047–7 (pbk.)
      1. Etiquette.   I. Title.
   BJ1853.L48   1998
   395—dc21   98–29053
                                                        CIP

To Adam and Cable.
Friendships that have taught me
manners are a sensitive awareness
to the feeling of others.

Contents

Acknowledgments

My father Arthur, stepmother Marilyn, and sister Patricia;

My hardworking office staff: Sharma Burke, David Dillon, Melissa Leister, Timothy Innes, Annie Jeeves, Kelly Kimball, Michael A. Norton, J. T. Steele, and Mondi Valiyee;

My long time literary agent and friend Alice Martell;

My loyal and wonderful friends: Adam Christing, Richard Imprescia, Karen Karsian, Nancy Mager, John McKillop, and Cable Neuhaus;

And special thanks to Jeff Cohen for his invaluable help and suport in developing this book.

INTRODUCTION

Why This Manners Book Is Different From All Other Manners Books

We have two regulatory systems: legal and etiquette. The legal system prevents us from killing each other. The etiquette system prevents us from driving each other crazy.

—JUDITH MARTIN (MISS MANNERS), interviewed by Kevin Kelly in *Wired* Magazine.

Ask the average person—although I've never met anyone in my life who was entirely average—what an entertainment publicist does, and they'll stammer a bit, and then usually make some guess about creating situations for celebrities to attract attention to themselves. They think being an entertainment publicist in the 1990s is akin to being someone's "press agent" in one of those 1940s movies, with the fedora, cigar, flashbulbs exploding in every direction, and a desk full of telephones, usually all ringing at once.

Well, except for the telephones, it's just not like that. Actually, being a publicist in the world of Hollywood is just like working in the "real" world—just more intense. On a daily basis I deal with some of the wealthiest, most powerful, charismatic, and creative people in the world—celebrities, agents, publishers, studio executives, entertainment attorneys, and managers. Their one common factor is that they require their publicist to get them through any number of difficult situations, with the best possible face on it, And that can range from lunch with a reporter to damage control after a publicity meltdown—you just never know.

Some of these people—albeit talented—are quite rude, and I have the psychic scars to prove it. This book is a compilation of the knowledge I have gleaned through the Etiquette School of Hard Knocks. It contains my own personal experience—a combination of knowledge, tact, sensitivity, good taste, and (hopefully) humor—which has helped me deal with just about all of life's situations and daily adventures. If this system works on the sharks of Hollywood, trust me, it'll work in your life too, even in difficult situations.

I'm not writing a book just to read my own words. I've gained a lot of experience in Hollywood, a place like no other on Earth, and that experience can be applied to life anywhere. The main thing is to pay attention to life as it happens.

So many people go through their lives on automatic pilot, and it's understandable. They have to get up in the morning, get themselves into some kind of presentable shape, help with their spouse, children, pets, get *them* out the door, and then make it to work themselves, where the desk is loaded with tasks to perform. We spend our days putting out fires, large and small, urgent but often not important, and then battle traffic or other commuters just to get home. It's no wonder our minds frequently focus on what happened yesterday or what's going to happen tomorrow, but so rarely on what's actually going on now, this minute, while we're driving our cars or riding the elevator or walking down the street to get a sandwich for lunch. Other people? What other people?

Being a publicist takes up a considerable amount of my life, but I try hard to be much more than just a publicist. I consider myself a keen observer of the way people live. I confess I am endlessly fascinated watching people, how they behave, and adjusting my own behavior to fit theirs or setting my behavior in opposition to theirs, to see how they will react. I am intensely curious about what makes people tick, why they do the things they do, and what I can learn as a result.

What I have learned so far is what I'm sharing in this book. Some of it is direct observation: what I've seen people do and what they've told me they've done. Some of it is my own opinion coming through—how I think people *should* treat each other and my theories as to why they do or don't. At times, it will be a combination of both, tempered by my own research into human behavior and the rules of society.

Society still does have rules, no matter how much we ignore them. If a business acquaintance passes you in the street without a greeting or a handshake, you wonder why he's violating that rule. If a man asks you out, seems to enjoy himself, says he'll call, and is never heard from again, his behavior is not acceptable within the rules of society. We think we understand our fellow humans until they break what we see as a rule, and then we wonder why they broke it.

I find social behavior fascinating. It offers unlimited opportunities to shine, to do the right thing, to make the right choice, to help you achieve what you want in life: love, monetary success, status, the admiration of your friends, coworkers, and family. But there is an equal number of chances (and ways) to mess up, embarrass yourself and others, destroy your reputation, and lose what you've worked for, and the difference between success and failure can often be as small as the amount of time it takes to say, "Thank you."

This book is designed to help you avoid some of the pitfalls, and I'm going to supply the road map to help you around them. Don't think though, that you're in safe hands because I was born with special etiquette knowledge, or a sense of exactly the right thing to do at any moment. No, you should be much more secure in reading this book knowing that I have made most of the mistakes I'll address—and often more than once.

The difference is, being an observer of life, I have noticed the mistakes as they've happened. I've forced myself to analyze them. I've tried to determine just where they came from, and do the same for others I've seen make them. That means I've managed to learn from my mistakes, and those mistakes I've observed—that's the difference.

So read on, with the confidence that you're being led by a man who has made mistakes you'll never make if you pay attention through this book. But be forewarned: I'm going to make you a participant in this process. You don't get to just sit there and nod your head at the words, you have to *think*. And sometimes, just to make sure you're listening, I'll throw in a pop quiz or a situation for you to solve yourself. You'll never know just where the next possible mistake might appear.

Just like life.

RAISE YOUR
SOCIAL I.Q.

1

Why Is Etiquette Necessary?

There is such a thing as manners! A way of treating people!

—Tom Cruise as Jerry Maguire,
written by Cameron Crowe

There are two axioms we hear repeated at various points in our lives: "rules are rules" and "rules are made to be broken." Clearly, these two sayings are at odds with each other. If rules are rules, and therefore must be obeyed because they're the rules, then how can they be made in order for us to break them? But they are central to the reasons we have rules to begin with.

Etiquette, after all, is a set of rules. Its purpose is not to make sure that everyone behaves the same way, but for everyone to know what the rules are, so that when they are broken, we can either condemn the rule breaker for breaking a rule ("rules are rules") or try to understand the reason for breaking it ("rules are made to be broken"). If there were no rules at all, everyone would behave randomly, and we would have no point of reference. One person you meet in the street might shake your hand in greeting, while another might spit in your face and mean the same thing. Rules are there as protection and as a signpost.

These days, however, etiquette is something that is often considered antiquated and obsolete. Etiquette is which fork to use at a dinner party, or how to address a wedding invitation to your college roommate and his wife. It includes rules that went out with horses and buggies. It seems to exist simply to shake a finger at us, to tell us what we're doing wrong and how boorish and uncivilized we've become. It doesn't offer solutions; it merely points out problems and shakes its head in disapproval.

So, then, why is etiquette necessary in the present day?

As I go through my day, I play any number of roles—publicist, friend, son, brother, mentor, author, among others. But the most important one is that of ambassador. And whether you know it or not, you're playing that very same role in your life.

What does an ambassador do? For example, an ambassador from another country comes to Washington for a conference, or to the United Nations for a debate. That ambassador represents his or her country; in essence, in the minds of the people he or she meets, the ambassador *is* the country, and the decisions made on the country's behalf. If the ambassador slams his hose on the table to gain attention, as Nikita Kruschev did at the United Nations in the 1950s, he might seem angry and unrefined, and his country will be perceived the same way. After all, they didn't let Kruschev into Disneyland.

When I meet someone for the first time, that person may only know a few rudimentary things about me. I'm a man; they can tell that by looking at me. Therefore, the things I do and the way I treat them will reflect in their minds as things that men do. I am, in a sense, an ambassador for men. If I treat this person badly, he or (especially) she may think this is something that a majority of men do, and harbor resentment toward men in their next relationship, be it professional or personal.

I'm also a Hollywood publicist, and that makes me an ambassador for the Hollywood community. Many people I meet have never been in contact with a movie star, studio, or production company. What they know about Hollywood is going to be based on what they find out about me. In my role as ambassador, I should be very careful about the way I represent my "country," Hollywood.

You do the same thing in your everyday life. If you're a woman, you act as an ambassador for all women as you deal with people in the course of your day. I'm also Jewish; therefore I am, whether I choose it or not, an ambassador for Jews when people meet me. Race, religion, sexual orientation, gender, occupation, and even hobbies can enter into normal conversations and relationships. If you're an in-line skater and you accidentally slam into someone walking because you're not paying attention to the road, you have made a bad impression for all skaters. Maybe you won't be recalled to your embassy, but you have made a negative impact on the world, however small.

That's where etiquette comes in. As a blueprint for social interaction, etiquette gives us common ground, a starting point on which to build our own rules. Maybe we won't follow every single rule to the letter; maybe we'll pick and choose among them to suit our own lifestyles. But we'd better know what the rules are or we'll be at a disadvantage. And in today's society being at a social disadvantage can mean loneliness, loss of income, depression, ostracism, and in some cases the death of a dream. It's easier to learn the rules than it is to suffer the consequences.

As ambassadors, we have a responsibility to represent our "country" well. As we've seen, our country can be anything from our gender to our business. When we're abroad, of course, we really do represent our country. The "ugly American" of the 1960s and 1970s is getting a somewhat more positive reputation, but there is still a long way to go.

When we meet someone—anyone—we ambassadors, are responsible for their first impression of us, as defined by the information they have about us. We need to remember that we're representing our "country," to make people feel good about our country, to make them want to meet and know other people from our country. The benefits we derive can include love, friendship, business advancement, and the overall knowledge that we've done something to make the world a little easier to live in for ourselves and someone else. That's no small feat.

So that seemingly irrelevant protocol, etiquette, takes on a new light when we see ourselves as ambassadors. After all, we don't want to make any mistakes when more than just our own reputation might be on the line. If we're concerned about how other people will be judged based on our own performance, we might pay a little more attention to detail. We need to be on top of our game to be sure that those who come after us will be well served.

The problem is that some of the rules of traditional etiquette really *are* outdated. Most of us don't have to worry about how to set a table for one hundred guests. Horses no longer roam the streets, so it doesn't matter if the man is on the curbside when a couple is walking along the sidewalk. Many of the rules passed down from decades ago assume that women are not working outside the home. They don't take into account fax machines, E-mail, and in some cases, telephones. They certainly don't talk much about sex.

What's needed, then, is an update. Not so much a rejection of the old rules as some revisions and additions. We don't need less etiquette these days; we need more. In a dating relationship, we have to know whether it's okay for the woman to call the man, whether an E-mail is as good as a note, whether it's too forward to have a spare toothbrush ready in the bathroom.

We also have to deal with the awkward situations that were traditionally swept under the rug or largely ignored by the accepted rules of etiquette. How do we react when a family member announces he's gay? What do we say to a friend who's suffered a devastating loss, or one who is terribly ill? What about the "morning after," when it's obvious that this relationship isn't going to work out?

First, you have to evaluate your level of readiness, what I like to call your Social I.Q. Take the following test, tally up your score, and you'll know where you stand. Then read the rest of the book, take the quiz at the end, and I'm willing to bet you'll end up with a higher score that will surprise you. Take the journey, and start with the first step. After all, every ambassador needs training.

YOUR SOCIAL I.Q. TEST

Answer each question honestly. Award yourself five points for every correct answer, and total your points at the end.

1. A business phone call should be returned:
   a. within the hour.
   b. the same day.
   c. the same week.
   d. whenever convenient.

Answer: B. Within an hour just isn't always possible, but the same day is the least you can do.

2. A personal phone call should be returned:
   a. within the hour.
   b. the same day.
   c. the same week.
   d. whenever convenient.

Answer: B. See above.

3. Thank-you notes are:
   a. an outdated formality.
   b. a quaint but unnecessary touch.
   c. an absolute necessity.
   d. none of the above

Answer: C. Thank you notes bring the most attractive quality—gratitude—to surface, and are the simplest, nicest and best way to express it.

4. E-mail is:
    a. not nearly as good as a personal note.
    b. as good as a personal note.
    c. better than a personal note, because it's faster.
    d. unacceptable.

Answer: A. While it is not absolutely rude, E-mail shows a rather cavalier attitude to communication—it's too convenient and easy. It's okay for chatting back and forth, but not as good as a personal note for thanks or serious communication.

5. For a first date:
    a. the man always calls the woman.
    b. the woman always calls the man.
    c. it doesn't matter who calls whom.
    d. women prefer men to call.

Answer: C. The person who gets the idea to go on a date should call. Gender isn't an issue.

6. On the "morning after," a man should:
    a. call the woman to reassure her he's still there.
    b. avoid calling the woman, so as not to appear pushy.
    c. send the woman a thank-you note.
    d. none of the above

Answer: A. Too many men get out of bed and into their cars, and are never heard from again. Calling just shows you're not one of them. Do it.

7. It's acceptable for a man to expect sex:
    a. after the third date.
    b. after the first date.
    c. after he proposes marriage.
    d. not necessarily any of the above

Answer: D. No one—male or female—should *expect* sex; it's something of a gift between two people. There's no set time limit; it should happen when both people want it to happen.

8. Letting your answering machine "screen" your phone calls is:
   a. perfectly acceptable.
   b. absolutely unacceptable.
   c. all right when you're busy.
   d. acceptable only when you're having sex.

Answer: A. There's nothing rude about having an answering machine. The key is when you return the call. Remember: the same day.

9. Your friend's mother has passed away. You say:
   a. "I'm so sorry."
   b. "Is your dad dating? I have this friend..."
   c. "Is there anything I can do to help?"
   d. "How much do you stand to inherit?"

Answer: C. You have nothing to be sorry about unless you're responsible. But you can offer to help in any way possible. If you answered b. or d., deduct five points from your score.

10. Someone in the locker room at the gym makes a racist remark. You:
   a. laugh along with the others and forget about it.
   b. get angry and start an argument.
   c. ignore the remark entirely.
   d. try to point out the offense in complimentary terms.

Answer: D. Going along is accepting the attitude, and you're part of the problem, not the solution. Ignoring it is the same as going along. Starting a fight isn't going to change your friend's attitude, and will lose you a friend. Read on for an explanation of the "Tiffany Theory." It will help with doing the right thing and keeping your friend.

11. Your relationship isn't working out. You:
   a. call up your partner and tell him or her it's over.
   b. send an E-mail.

    c. insist on meeting face-to-face, even if that means causing a difficult emotional scene.

    d. send a letter of regret and good-bye.

Answer: C. Telephone, E-mail or written "Dear John" letters show a lack of respect and cowardice. Be a grown-up; face your partner and explain it in the best way you can.

12. A co-worker you've never considered romantically unexpectedly asks you out. You:

    a. say you never mix business with dating.

    b. smile tolerantly and evade the question.

    c. accept even if you don't want to.

    d. none of the above

Answer: D. Don't say you never mix business with dating, because someone you may want to go out with could be listening. The best thing: be honest and say you're not interested in that kind of relationship with this person, but that you're flattered.

13. A close friend says he's very ill. Your reaction:

    a. "Does this mean you're going to die?"

    b. "What can I do to help?"

    c. "Does that mean your wife's available?"

    d. none of the above

Answer: B. Much like Question 9, this is a situation that can be painful no matter what you do. Don't make it worse by concentrating on yourself; your friend is the one who needs you. Offer whatever help you can.

14. Your brother announces he's gay. You:

    a. tell him you always suspected.

    b. ask him not to come near your children.

    c. banish him from your home.

    d. offer support in dealing with the family.

Answer: D. You get two points for a., but only if you really have always suspected; don't lie. If you answered b. or c., you need this and many other books to help you through your problem. The family could be difficult; offer help.

15. You've had an explosive argument with your sister, and Thanksgiving is coming up. You:
    a. arrange to have the holiday with your spouse's family.
    b. face your sister and have it out in front of the whole family.
    c. sit across the table from her, silent and stony.
    d. be pleasant and try to arrange a time when you can talk candidly on another day.

Answer: D. Avoiding problems is better than having to resolve them. In this case, talking before the event and trying to make peace is the best thing. If not, try a., but only give yourself two points.

16. You just broke up with a lover after a six-month relationship. Until now, you have been a member of the health club where she works. Is it best now to:
    a. give up the expensive membership to avoid uncomfortable confrontations.
    b. keep going to work out, but try to avoid her area.
    c. keep going, and act as if nothing's changed.
    d. none of the above

Answer: B. It's silly to give up the membership fee, but good taste to try and avoid the object of a painful relationship. It's better for both of you.

17. Your parents are divorcing, and your father keeps calling to have long talks in which he complains bitterly about your mother. You:
    a. act the good child and listen to his complaints dutifully.
    b. defend your mother and start an argument.
    c. ask that he stop making those remarks to you, and risk his feeling he can't talk candidly to you.
    d. none of the above

Answer: C. You want to be loyal to your father, but you have a responsibility to your mother, too. Be the best child to each of them during this difficult time. Avoid ugly remarks, and offer support to both parents. Don't ever agree that anyone was the wrong party; it'll just come back to haunt you.

18. Your friends' child has just interrupted the adults' conversation one time too many, and their parents are not correcting the child. You:
    a. say nothing, but make a mental note not to invite your friends with their children again.
    b. correct the child in front of the parents.
    c. wait for the child to leave the room, then tell the parents you think his behavior is rude.
    d. laugh it off and forget the whole thing.

Answer: C. It's never appropriate to discipline another person's child when the parent is present; it's their job. But it is acceptable to let the parents know that you don't tolerate some kinds of behavior in your own home.

19. A woman you dated once has been calling every day for three weeks. You're not interested in seeing her again, but she won't take a hint. You:
    a. take the umpteenth phone call and tell her as nicely as possible that you're not interested.
    b. put the answering machine on "screen."
    c. send her a note explaining your feelings.
    d. hire a bodyguard.

Answer: A. Persistence will out. Anything else is either callous or cowardly; go ahead and explain it again. Preferably in person, but only the first time. After that, the phone is acceptable.

20. A business acquaintance has been making comments about getting together on the weekend to go rock climbing. As a business acquaintance, he's okay, but you're not sure he's "friend material." You:

    a. tell him you're busy and hope he takes the hint.
    b. go once because you've always wanted to rock climb.
    c. ignore it until he sets an actual date.
    d. any of the above

Answer: D. Any one of the above is acceptable. But only do b. if you're sure you're really interested in the activity, not because you're trying to be polite; it'll send out the wrong signal.

21. You had a great time on your date, and you want to invite him in, but your eight-year-old daughter will be sleeping in the next room, and you're uncomfortable with it. You:
    a. ask him to make plans for another night when your daughter has a sleep-over.
    b. make plans for another "date" at a local hotel or his place.
    c. invite him in and try to be quiet.
    d. none of the above

Answer: A. There's nothing wrong with sex between two consenting adults, and every couple has to have a first time if they're going to have a time at all. But it's understandable to be concerned about a child involved with one parent; keep your hormones in check until you're not in danger of harming another emotional life.

22. A former coworker, who was fired from her job, keeps inviting herself along when the "gang" goes to lunch. You:
    a. keep your mouth shut and hope someone else tells her it's uncomfortable.
    b. tell her yourself and risk insulting her.
    c. start choosing a new place to eat, so she won't find you there.
    d. try to find her a new job.

Answer: B. Somebody has to be the responsible adult here. If everyone is uncomfortable with the situation, letting it go on longer isn't going to help. Step up to the plate and take a swing.

23. E-mail is better than a phone call when:
  a. you need to choose your words perfectly, and a letter would be too slow.
  b. you're afraid a voice-to-voice encounter would result in an unpleasant confrontation.
  c. your friend is a devoted techno-geek.
  d. never

Answer: A. Both criteria must be in play. If there's a need for speed, and you're afraid you won't be diplomatic with your words, opt for E-mail. But not in personal relationships or when a face-to-face meeting is necessary. Don't use your computer as a screen to hide behind.

24. Honesty is *not* the best policy when:
  a. it will get you fired.
  b. it is hurtful.
  c. you can lose your lover.
  d. never

Answer: B. It's not great to get fired, either, but a lie will probably be found out. If the truth is truly going to hurt, try to find a way to say nothing.

25. When honesty will hurt, but it's necessary:
  a. say it as quickly as you can to get it over with.
  b. do it face-to-face.
  c. try and say something positive before and after the difficult part.
  d. all of the above

Answer: D. The Tiffany Theory, coupled with issues of civility and simple consideration. You have so much to learn. Keep reading.

Score

  0–20: Don't move before reading the rest of this book!
  25–50: You can go to the fridge, but don't talk to anybody before reading the rest of this book.

55–75: Read this book at bedtime, but don't take more than a week to do it.

80–100: You still have to read, but take your time.

105–120: Hey, you're good. Just read the chapters with titles that interest you.

125: Would you consider collaborating, ambassador?

WHY SOCIETY IS LESS POLITE THAN IT USED TO BE

I feel that if a person can't communicate, the very least he can do is to shut up.

—TOM LEHRER

There's little question that life is rougher than it used to be, even with all the technological advances that have been made. Sure, we have E-mail, but we also have carpal tunnel syndrome. We have CDs, but we have to deal with AIDS, terrorism, poverty, illiteracy, property taxes, hair loss, and the designated hitter. It hardly seems fair.

Baby boomers, who constitute an enormous percentage of the population, grew up with a bang. Most of us remember where we were when John F. Kennedy was shot, and it created a very strong sense in us that nothing was safe, and nothing was fair. In subsequent years, the assassinations of Martin Luther King Jr., Robert Kennedy, and John Lennon, perhaps the symbol of our generation, reinforced those feelings.

It's no wonder, then, that people are less friendly than they used to be. If we can't count on anything and if everything we know is in peril, we might be just a little bit more guarded in our dealings with other people. If we're concerned that the stranger next to us may be violent with absolutely no provocation, it makes sense that we're not overly concerned with giving him an amiable smile.

Many of us, too, came of age in the 1960s, when flaunting the rules was, well, the rule. Everything that had come before us seemed dated and silly, and telling the Establishment what it could do with its rules was all the rage. We wore clothes, grew hair, and said things that were guaranteed to give our parents anxiety attacks. And we reveled in it.

Even for those of us who didn't continue on with the politics of the 1960s, those early lessons were ingrained. There was no reason to follow rules unless we agreed with them. There was no reason to believe that things that were here with us now could be counted on to be here with us tomorrow. There was no reason to conform to formalities.

Given all that, it's easy to understand why etiquette became a comic idea, and why following rules just because they were rules seemed like the most ridiculous thing one could do. Even Judith Martin had to take the pseudonym Miss Manners and adopt an exaggerated style of speaking and writing to get the message of politeness across—she adopted a persona that made fun of itself while it managed to put at least some of the rules of etiquette back into discussion.

What's not easy to understand is why the tide of rude and coarse behavior has gone as far as it has. Informality is one thing, but it's quite another to be outwardly hostile to everyone you meet. Maybe all the rules don't need to be followed to the letter, but shouldn't one—do unto others as you would have them do unto you—still hold?

Every day, we see more evidence that there is a desperate need for etiquette. Drive on any major highway in any part of the country, and you'll see what I mean. Bumper stickers carry slogans that parents don't want to explain to their children; drivers make gestures at each other that wouldn't be permissible on network television; people actually risk death or serious injury in order to get ahead of each other and arrive at a destination seconds sooner than the next guy. And that's just during the morning commute.

As the day progresses, we see more of the same. Coworkers pass each other in the hall and barely grunt in lieu of a hello;

your lunch date cancels at 11:45; half your calls aren't returned; the man you dated last night doesn't call; the woman you're seeing cancels dinner without an explanation; your sister calls to complain about your mother; your father calls to remind you of the family reunion next Sunday but doesn't ask how your husband is; your boss forgets your name...and it's not even noon yet.

To some extent, it's easy to understand all these minor slights. Everyone else is having a hard day, too. Their morning commute was just as bad as yours. Their newspaper was thrown in the bushes again. Their kids also have to go from school to soccer practice to dance class to kung fu to bar mitzvah lessons. They're just as cranky as you are. It's easy to understand. But that doesn't mean it has to be accepted.

I believe the toxic effects of bad behavior are just as dangerous as those of secondhand smoke, and they're being ignored. If people don't know how to treat each other or don't care how they treat each other, our society is damaged. And when you multiply that damage by the millions, or hundreds of millions nationwide, you can see that the problem is nothing less than the survival of our society as we know it. Maybe not in the literal sense, but certainly in the spiritual one.

We are worn down, little by little, and as we interact with each other, we are exhausted collectively. The effect is the same as the hole in the ozone layer—it deteriorates our atmosphere and makes it harder for us to live on the planet. And the solution is the same: We have to reverse the damage we've done to ourselves before it's too late.

That's not easy. It's one thing to resolve to treat everyone we meet better, but to remember that when we get cut off in the left lane or the person ahead of us in the express aisle has more than eight items in his cart is another thing entirely. The saving grace is etiquette. If we know the rules and practice them, they become second nature.

Once we start practicing them and doing so out of habit, maybe some of the people we meet will do the same. If they do, perhaps some of the people *they* meet will continue the trend.

Before you know it (all right, maybe not before you know it, but soon), the majority of us could be acting—out of sheer habit—more civil to everyone we know, and *that* can spread just like secondhand smoke. But the effect it has will be the reverse—it will make people live longer and more satisfying lives.

Does that mean that we have to go back to engraved invitations to lunch, gentlemen shielding ladies from the curbside splashes of horse-drawn carriages, and curtsies? Of course not. But it does mean that we can return to treating others the way we would have them treat us. After all, that is the one thing we can be sure everyone wants.

The question is, how do we do that when the real-life conditions of the modern era throw a decidedly difficult situation in our path? The key to almost every awkward moment is to remember that one rule: How would you want this person to treat you if your roles were reversed? If you can put yourself in the other person's shoes for a moment, think how they must feel, and set aside how uncomfortable you are, you will have a very good head start on virtually any curve life throws at you.

That sounds easier than it actually is. Put yourself in another person's situation? When you're feeling uncomfortable, perhaps angry, maybe intimidated? Set your feelings aside when society has spent decades telling us that our feelings are the most important thing in the world? Undo years of training that make us distrustful, even resentful, of our fellow man?

That's what etiquette is for, to make it common practice to put yourself in another's position—and that's why you need to start trying right now. Think of the last argument you had with someone. No matter how unreasonable the other person might have seemed, can you understand why he or she felt that way? Why couldn't that person see things the way you saw them? Couldn't they put themselves in your shoes?

If you can find a way into that person's head, to understand what their point of view might have been, then you have an idea of what the argument might *really* have been about. Could it have been avoided? Perhaps. But perhaps not. In any case, entering the other persons psyche gives you practice in the art of etiquette. The next time something like that happens, try to put yourself in the other person's place *when it happens*. It's possible you might be able to avoid another unpleasant argument.

That's what etiquette in the present day is all about—finding a way past all the distractions modern life places in our way to find common ground. Once you can do that, you will have a handle on every awkward situation that confronts you. There are, of course, different ways to achieve that goal. Based on the circumstances that surround it, each situation will require a separate solution. Read on, and you'll get an idea of how to avoid awkward situations before they arise, and to deal with the ones that do manage to make their way into your day.

It's not hard; it's just a question of practice and dedication.

THE TIFFANY THEORY

Everything looks worse in black-and-white.
> —Paul Simon, from the lyrics to "Kodachrome"

It's interesting that since he recorded "Kodachrome" in 1972, Paul Simon has changed the lyrics to: "everything looks better in black-and-white." It's a question of illusion versus reality, and the illusion goes from being the too-bright color images of Kodak film to the black-and-white movies of a more innocent time. Everything does, indeed, look better in black-and-white. Humphrey Bogart sacrifices the woman he loves for the good of the Allied cause, and looks great doing it. Things seemed a heck of a lot easier in those days.

Illusion, or at least appearance, plays a role in most decisions made by people with sight. We choose our mates first by how they look; after all, if someone is completely unattractive to us, it's unlikely we will strike up a conversation with them, let alone start a romance. And while it is indeed a mistake to judge a book by its cover, it's also significant to notice that everyone is usually trying to look as good as they can.

That's where the Tiffany Theory of human interaction comes in. Let's say you receive a gift from someone you know relatively well, but not intimately. The gift comes wrapped in paper which bears the name, Kmart. You might note that it was nice of your friend to send you a gift, but you probably won't be so excited that you can't wait to tear off the paper and find out what's inside the box.

Now, take the same gift, from the same person, and substitute Tiffany's logo for Kmart's. Suddenly the gift is much more interesting, and you pay much more attention to it as you quickly try to discern exactly what could be inside. Your estimation of the gift-giver might even rise somewhat. It's certain that the Tiffany logo will command more cachet than the Kmart one, even if the box holds precisely the same item (granted, it's unlikely that you'll receive a Tiffany spice rack or a Kmart pendant, but in gifts it's the thought that counts, isn't it?).

What does this have to do with etiquette? Plenty.

Here's a situation you don't want to happen to you, but it does. You're finished working out at the gym, and in the locker room, while you're drying off from your shower, you hear a friend talking to a group of men you may or may not know. Your friend uses a racial slur in a joke, and the men laugh.

Do you laugh along, and tacitly endorse the ugly racial word? Do you confront your friend and let him know that you don't care for that sort of language? Do you wait until later? Let's examine your options.

Option 1: You can pretend to find the joke amusing and literally laugh the whole thing off.

The upside of this option is that you can totally avoid the unpleasant situation of confronting your friend's racism and your disgust with the subject. Your friend stays your friend, there's no ugly scene, and nobody, it seems, gets hurt.

Of course, there's also a downside. If the language bothers you enough, you're going to be beating yourself up emotionally over your failure to act. Worse than that, there will be more of it in the future, for sure—not to mention that your friend doesn't confront his racism. He may display it again, and if the circumstances are different, he could end up either causing or getting into serious trouble. By avoiding a confrontation, you may be failing to resolve the situation and helping to perpetuate it.

Also keep in mind that this chapter is about perceptions. If you chuckle along with the rest of the guys in the locker room, you're delivering the message that you approve of racist remarks, and coloring the perception that everyone in the room has of *you*. In this case, the downside greatly outweighs the upside. You can't do nothing.

Option 2: In front of all the other men, you can confront your friend in the locker room, telling him you think that remark was racist, in bad taste, and destructive, and that you won't put up with that kind of talk in your presence.

Now, this clearly addresses the problem of the perception everyone else in the room has of *you*. You are making it clear that you do not tolerate racial slurs and presenting yourself as a moral and courageous person. It may even help with the other men in the room.

The downsides? Plenty. First of all, you're not taking your friend's feelings into account. Being publicly brought to task isn't anyone's idea of a good time, and you could very well be sacrificing a friendship for a moral and political principle. Maybe you think this is cause enough to do so, but maybe you don't.

Also, the other men in the room might agree with your friend's point of view, and in that case the only thing you'll end up doing is alienating everyone in the room, leaving yourself open to ridicule and cementing their views on the subject if you sound shrill and silly. But that's not the worst part.

The worst part is that all your effort on your friend's behalf will most likely be for naught. People don't generally take well to being dressed down in front of friends or acquaintances. They tend to shut down, tune out your message, and pay attention to other things, like how angry they are. You won't be getting your message across to your friend because he'll be too mad at you to hear you, and that is where the Tiffany Theory enters the discussion.

Option 3: Picture your message—your disgust at a tasteless race joke—as a gift. If that gift is wrapped in paper from Kmart, that is, if you deliver it bluntly, telling your friend that you think he's behaved like a racist and a fool, he is unlikely to be listening by the time you finish your first sentence. But, if you deliver your message in paper from Tiffany's, you have a much better chance of getting it heard.

First, say something kind about your friend: "I know you're a very kind and caring person. I know you're upset by injustice and unfairness. It's part of the reason I consider you such a dear friend." Then explain that his behavior wasn't true to all that you know about him; that he gave an impression of himself that was different from his real persona; that if a stranger walked into the room he would have assumed your friend was a terrible racist and a rude, insensitive person. Finish with something else positive—the gift wrapping on the other side of the box—that reassures your friend that you still feel the same way about him as before, but that he should be more careful about his behavior.

Using the Tiffany Theory, it's considerably more likely that your friend will get the message. Even if he's offended in the beginning, you have presented your information in the most positive light you can, and it's likely your friend will come around. You have achieved as many of your goals as you possibly could: alerting your friend to his behavior, telling him it offends you and why, and possibly making him think before he uses racist language again. It's an awkward situation, but you've managed to make the best of it. And that is what etiquette is all about.

THE TEN COMMANDMENTS OF A SOCIAL I.Q.

1. Thou shalt return telephone calls promptly.
2. Thou shalt send thank you notes, and instruct thy children to do the same.
3. Thou shalt RSVP to all invitations before the specified date.

4. Thou shalt call or send a note after a date, whether thou intends to keep seeing the person or not.
5. Thou shalt bring a small gift when visiting someone's home.
6. Thou shalt not ask embarrassing questions, like, "Did you have a facelift?"
7. Thou shalt not substitute E-mail for a written note.
8. Thou shalt make eye contact.
9. Thou shalt choose thy words carefully, especially in awkward situations.
10. Thou shalt be grateful and empathize.

WE ARE ALL TEACHERS, HEALERS AND MINISTERS

We cannot solve life's problems except by solving them.
—M. Scott Peck, *The Road Less Traveled*

It's not enough to look at the world and shake your head at what it's become. It's not enough to bemoan modern times and think back to the "good old days" when things were simpler and purer. It's not enough to look at the problems of others and say, "Thank goodness that's not my problem." It *is* yours, too.

The world has become meaner. The toxic energy put out by decades of eroding civility is making everyone in the United States more self-centered and ungrateful, and the situation is getting worse with each passing day. With such overwhelming odds, it often seems that there's nothing we can do about the awful problems facing the world: racism, sexism, political upheaval, violence. Something like manners seems so removed from those huge issues that they couldn't possibly be connected. In fact, they are connected as strongly as they can be, and if we improve the state of manners, if we increase the civility with which we deal with each other, we will take huge strides toward solving, or at least improving, the others.

We are all teachers, healers, and ministers. I am, you are. We go through our lives teaching those who have less experience than ourselves. We heal, although most of us do not practice medicine. Mothers and fathers help children feel better. Friends can help heal psychic wounds and emotional pain. We can all go through our days making life more pleasant for virtually everyone we meet. It's a question of recognizing our opportunities and deciding to take advantage of them.

Teacher

In very general terms, you can teach something to virtually everyone you meet every day. Keep in mind that much of what we learn comes from the examples set by others.

- If you return a telephone call within the hour you receive it, your call to that person is likely to be returned promptly next time.
- If you respond to someone's invitation, that person is more likely to RSVP when you invite them to an event.
- If you are kind to a grieving friend, that friend will probably remember your generous gesture when you are in a time of need.
- If you can defuse a tense situation with some welcome good humor, the people you help relax may do the same for you, or someone else, when a similar situation arises.
- If you take the time to learn the religious customs of a friend before attending a wedding, or other ceremony, in their place of worship, you go a long way toward reducing your natural unease in an unfamiliar situation, it will also set an example for others from outside the faith who attend, and make a statement to your friend that you are willing to learn about something that is important to her.

Of course, it is important to teach children, but adults in today's society need just as much education in the art of dealing politely with each other. The better the example you set, the better lesson you teach, and the benefit of simply feeling better about yourself is an additional plus.

One other thing: don't try to teach someone something that you haven't mastered yourself. If you're only up to this chapter in this book, you're not ready to teach Social I.Q. yet, you have to keep reading. By the same token, if you just started studying art, religion, Japanese, or cooking, you can't teach them to someone else so soon. Wait until you've acquired a skill before you start sharing it.

Healer

It's one thing to go to medical school and become a physician. Some people do it because they hope to go into a lucrative profession.others out of the desire to help their fellow human beings.still others from a combination of the two, or for other reasons. But you don't have to graduate from Johns Hopkins to be a healer; you can even practice without a license.

The key is to distinguish *medicine* from *healing*. Medicine is something that must be practiced by trained professionals, while healing is something that anyone can do. It doesn't require medical training, only common sense and a good heart. And by that I don't mean a strong cardiac muscle, but the ability to empathize and feel compassion for another person. Healing doesn't have to be a physical process.

Many people you see every day are suffering, and only a few are suffering from physical ailments. Some are in emotional pain over events in their lives, some are in psychic pain over the actions of long-gone relatives or childhood traumas. Some are suffering from the toxic effects of our society. You can help them. Does this mean that you should practice psychiatry without a license? Of course not, no more than I'm suggesting that you should practice surgery, prescribe medication, or diagnose illnesses. What we're discussing here is the ability that we all have to make other people feel better about themselves (and, as a side benefit, us) by treating them with the kind of respect and compassion we all deserve.

This just doesn't happen enough in the modern world. At work, we are treated like pieces of a machine, like servants and functionaries at home, and like Hollywood extras by the rest of the world (just walk by, and don't say anything or it will cost the production money). We all deserve compassion and empathy. Empathy is key. Where some people use the axiom that you should "step into someone else's shoes," I think you should put yourself inside another person's hat. After all, once you're inside someone's head, you can understand what makes him happy, what troubles him, what makes him feel sad, angry, frustrated, hopeless, ecstatic—whatever. But you have to develop your own natural ability to feel what the other person feels.

This is not a New Age or ESP concept. I don't expect you to be able to read my thoughts or those of anyone else (most of us have enough problems with our *own* thoughts to even consider reading someone else's). It's not a magical power. It's something that we all have, but we need to recognize and develop it in order to make it work.

Actors have a tool called motivation, which they learn about in their most rudimentary classes. In every role they play, actors will constantly be concerned about their character's motivation. What makes him or her act the way they do? Some actors go so far as to imagine what they call elaborate back stories for their characters; they start at birth and determine every significant event that went on for these characters, leading up to the time of the story being told in the play or movie.

That's what you need to do. Consider another person's motivation. What makes her act like that? Why would she do such a thing? Does she realize the implications of what she's saying or doing? Think beyond your own emotions, especially if you're involved in an argument or in some way in conflict with this person. You can't allow anger to cloud your judgment. Think hard. If you understand the motivation for a behavior, you can help heal the person of the problem that is causing it.

Sometimes it's simply a question of pointing out what you think the motivation is. You tell the person in question what you believe is causing him to act in an inappropriate way. This has to be coupled with the Tiffany Theory—if you start with an argumentative, combative attitude, it's not very likely the person will listen to your message. But start with positive comments and then explain what you think the problem is, and your odds increase dramatically.

Of course, sometimes the person you're dealing with will not react well to the information you're trying to convey, no matter how well you present it. Remember, you're a healer, not a debater. You have to empathize with your friend, put yourself in his hat, and don't fight back. Tell him you understand, that you've felt the same way before yourself, and here's something that has worked for you. More times than not, if you're patient and make it clear that you're trying to help, you will help your friend heal. There's no better feeling on earth.

Minister

What does a minister do? Well, a minister generally tries to help people through the more difficult passages of life—grief, loss, spiritual confusion, illness. Of course, most ministers do their good deeds in the context of one religion or another, but you can be a lay minister in your dealings with other people, and you don't need to go to divinity school.

Once again, it's important to note that you should not do what someone with years of training and experience does. You're not a real minister, but you can act as one in everyday situations in the same way you act as a teacher and a healer. Adapt to the situation, and do what someone who cares should do.

When someone you know is suffering through a hard time, it's especially important to be empathetic. You have to imagine what the other person feels and try to remember a time when you might have felt the same way. To help you empathize, use your own experience the way actors do. You can apply it to your friend's situation, but don't explain that to your friend unless he asks. Telling other people about a time when you had similar troubles doesn't help them with theirs unless you have a very practical solution that can help them now. Just making the point

Mr. Watson to come into the room. Of course, Bell had spilled acid onto his lap and may be forgiven for being in somewhat of a hurry.

Unfortunately, that first conversation was seen as a precedent. People have since taken Bell's opening words and found countless additional ways to be uncivil on the phone. In fact, these days it is the rare person who is polite on the telephone when they're not trying to sell you something.

You may have noticed that in previous chapters, I have made a number of references to returning phone calls. There's a good reason for that. There are few things that seem to me as inexcusable as not returning a phone call, and returning it *promptly*. In my business, I am known as being somewhat obsessive on the subject, and my reputation is well earned, but I think with very good cause.

If someone is taking time out of their day to pick up a telephone and call you—be it for business or personal reasons—it is simply common courtesy to return that phone call, should you not be available to speak when the phone rings. There's no excuse for not returning a call, especially in this age of communications technology, when people are rarely more than a few feet (if that) from a telephone. You can find the time.

In my office we have a rule, and it is strictly adhered to: every call, every day. That means that every single call which comes into the office is returned the same day, either by myself or by someone working with me. We don't leave until those calls are answered, and if one comes in while we're leaving, we deal with it then. Nobody goes unanswered until the next day. Nobody. Not the president of a movie studio and not the janitor. I can't emphasize that point too strongly.

Along with advancing technology have come any number of awkward situations related to the telephone and its use. Let's have a quick pop quiz (don't forget, I warned you in the introduction), and see how well you do:

1. You have call waiting. You're on the phone with a friend
   and expecting a call from another friend. Sure enough, just
   when your friend is talking about her sad love life, the little
   beep is heard. You:
   a. tell your first friend you have to go and get off.
   b. click over to your second friend and tell him you
       can't talk now, but will call back later.
   c. ignore the beep and make a mental note to call your
       second friend when you get off the phone.
   d. any of the above

Answer: C. Call waiting is mechanized rudeness in a nutshell.
I prefer not to have it, but there are times when it's a business
necessity. Given its inevitability, as a necessary evil, it's best to
ignore the little tone when you're not expecting an absolutely
vital call. Telling a person you're talking to that you prefer to
talk to someone else is unspeakably rude. Telling the person
who's calling that the first person is more important to you at
this moment is almost as bad. Letting the second friend hear the
phone ring with no answer isn't rude, they'll call back later if it's
important. And since you're going to call back promptly
yourself (that's essential), you can keep everybody happy—even
yourself.

2. You are working at home and the telephone rings. You let
   the answering machine pick up the call, but then you hear
   your mother's voice leaving a message. It is polite to:
   a. pick up as she's leaving a message, letting her know
       you were screening calls.
   b. let her leave the message, then call back immediately,
       saying you just came in.
   c. let her leave the message, then call back in an hour to
       give the impression you were out?

Answer: B. Call screening can lead to serious, and sometimes
unintentional, rudeness. The best thing to do is to allow the
machine to do its job. Don't inform the caller that you were
screening out unwanted calls (since the caller will then wonder

if you're screening her out whenever the answering machine picks up), but call back as soon as you can.

3. You're in your office; your boss is in his. He's receiving a call on his speakerphone, and you're aware of it because you can hear him from your cubicle, which is half a room away. You:
    a. keep your mouth shut because he's the boss and you could get fired.
    b. tell him in no uncertain terms that he's interfering with all the work he's hired you and others to do.
    c. go into his office after the call is through and say, "I'll bet you didn't know this, but we can hear your speakerphone all the way out in the bullpen."

Answer: C. Okay, this was an easy one. But it's important to note that the Tiffany Theory applies here, as well. Starting with "I'll bet you didn't know this..." does two things: it gives the boss an excuse for his inconsiderate behavior, and it shows him that you think well enough of him to assume he doesn't know when he's being inconsiderate. If he continues to do this after you've spoken with him, say nothing (see A).

4. It's the day after your first date with a woman you'd like to see again. It is:
    a. too soon to call her again, so as not to appear desperate.
    b. exactly the time to call again, since the fine time you both had is fresh in your minds.
    c. neither of the above

Answer: B. It's not the timing of the call that matters, it's the tone. If you sound so needy that you convince the woman you're going to be an emotional sponge, absorbing but giving nothing back, you're on the wrong course, but if you simply want to continue a relationship that appears to have potential, there's no time like the present.

5. The phone rings, and when you pick it up, there is a computer-generated voice on the line; this is clearly going to be a sales call. Keeping in mind that we want to raise the level of manners in the world generally, you:

a. wait patiently until the sales operator picks up and explain that you're not interested in the product she's selling.

b. wait impatiently until the sales operator picks up, and before she has a chance to explain what she's selling, ask pointedly for her to remove you from her phone list immediately.

c. hang up on the computer.

Answer: C. Trick question. You don't have to be polite to machines.

This quick quiz was meant to give you an idea of the problems technology has wrought, and also to empower you with solutions. Whenever a sticky telephone situation arises, think Is there a way I can get what I want out of this development *without hurting anyone's feelings?* If there is, by all means, use it.

After all, you're entitled to be satisfied, too. Keep in mind what Oliver Herford once said: "A gentleman is one who never hurts anyone's feelings unintentionally." Civility is the art of not hurting someone's feelings when meaning only to satisfy your own desires in the situation. The more awkward the situation, the more civility you need to exhibit. But your needs are important, too. They're just not the *only* important consideration.

The telephone may be the epicenter of etiquette in the modern age (although the computer is coming up fast on the outside). It provides great utility, the ability to speak to virtually any person in civilization at any moment, and the ability to communicate feelings and information directly, person-to-person. But there are dangers: telephones can also be instruments of incivility, intentional or otherwise. With every ring of the phone, there is the potential for joy or insult. Use at your own risk, but boost your Social I.Q. whenever you pick up the receiver.

Keep in Mind

- Returning phone calls promptly is absolutely essential.
- Call waiting is to be used only when absolutely necessary.
- Call screening, although sometimes necessary, is best used discreetly.
- Use your speakerphone only when you have to, and at a low volume.

2

The Office

BUSINESS SITUATIONS

Be neat, discreet, and keep your ear to the ground.
> —THE MAMAS AND THE PAPAS,
> from the lyrics to "Free Advice"

Thirty years ago, "business" was something practiced by a special group of people, "businessmen." They generally wore white shirts and ties, went to "the office" and "did business." They were almost exclusively men, usually white men, and interacted mostly with each other. They kept the supposed secrets of "business" to themselves.

The rest of us, or our parents, went to "work." They had a "job," which paid them a salary. They wore various kinds of clothing, depending on the job, and while they were still more often than not men, they discussed their jobs with pretty much anyone, often as a topic of daily conversation around the dinner table It was clear that "business" and a "job" were two different things, and the people involved in each rarely saw or spoke to each other.

Things have changed.

Especially in the past fifteen years, the concept of work has changed radically in the United States and around the world. Technology certainly has had a lot to do with that change. The greatly increased access to the Internet, for example, has made it much easier for people to work at home, creating the word *telecommuter*. And fax machines, telephones, E-mail, and overnight delivery services have made it much simpler for businesses to communicate with each other quickly. That, in turn, has made it much easier and less expensive for people to start their own businesses from home. For a large percentage of the population these days, their "business" is themselves.

In addition to the increase in self-employed people, it's a well-documented fact that business no longer stands as the exclusive domain of males. In fact, women make up at least an equal percentage of the work force in America. Out of financial necessity, most women, even those married and with children, have to work to help support the family. Many of them work because they want to, some because they simply have to. Single mothers work, so do married women without children.

In business the rules of etiquette haven't really changed because of these shifts in the workplace, but they have become important to more people than ever before, because more people are involved in business. Like everything else in the modern age, too, technology has complicated the etiquette of the workplace. For one thing, it has made it possible for the workplace to be in the middle of the living room. But technology is the chief means of communication in all aspects of life these days, and business is probably the leading example of that fact.

Think about that: technology is the chief means of communication. That means that most of the time we're communicating, it's through a telephone, a fax machine, a computer, or some other technological gadget. What once seemed like science fiction to our parents has become our waking nightmare, since the rules of communicating are getting more, not less, complicated with each silicon-chipped advance.

After considerable thought, I've come to conclude that technology is the enemy of reverence. The more dependent on machines and microchips we become, the less civil and reverent our culture grows. It is a dangerous trend, and one that can only be overcome with strict attention to the rules of decent behavior that your Social I.Q. helps you practice, because if you think awkward situations arise in personal relationships, you ain't seen nothin' yet. Business is fraught with pitfalls, places to go wrong, and people who sincerely want to see you fail. You do the wrong thing at any time, and you can find yourself in an even more awkward situation—unemployed.

Does that mean you have to be completely ruthless, cold-hearted, and cruel in order to survive? On the contrary. Remember your role as an ambassador—you need to be a representative of your business when you interact with other people, and that will help you just as well in your chosen profession as in any other area of life. In fact, it's more important to be careful with your Social I.Q. in business, because business is never entirely separate from social situations. The people with whom you work may be your friends; one of them could become a lover, spouse, or an ally when you need one. As a person whose business relies very heavily on skills in social situations, let me tell you firsthand: manners are desperately important in the business community.

Can situations be awkward? More than ever. Are the stakes high? Absolutely. Are the rewards great? They can be. So how does one navigate the sea of business with an eye toward civil and mannerly behavior with all one meets? Let's take an awkward-situation-by-awkward-situation approach and see what develops. After all, business is quite often conducted on the spur of the moment, you have to be prepared all the time. In the next few chapters, I'll present some awkward business situations, along with suggestions on how to deal with them. But don't think of these solutions as the only way to behave, or these situations as the only ones in which thinking quickly and maintaining your manners will serve you in business; they are meant to be archetypes, examples. What I'm about to tell you can be applied to all business situations, even those we can't anticipate for this book and those that are specific to your business. It just takes a little practice (okay, a *lot* of practice) and the ability to improvise—just a little.

Don't be afraid. No awkward situations can arise while you're reading a book.

MEETINGS

> *A committee is a group that keeps minutes and loses hours.*
>
> —Milton Berle

There is another quote, attributed to various people and apparently older than the Hollywood hills, that goes something like: "A camel is a horse that was designed by a committee." Anyone who has ever been to any business meeting consisting of more than one person will attest to the truth of that statement.

Still, business meetings are unavoidable, and, in fact, can be useful when they have a purpose and the people attending address it. In fact, most business meetings are necessary to at least some of the people who attend them, and can be very helpful tools toward building a stronger business, career, product, or service. The trick is learning how to make the meetings accomplish the tasks for which they were scheduled.

You might be surprised by this, but behaving in a civil and polite manner at business meetings can actually help them reach their goals. Behaving properly can certainly score you points with those who supervise you, and might help to advance you up the corporate ladder in some small fashion. But like anything else—in fact, perhaps *more* than anything else—business meetings have their own protocol, their own set of rules, and there's no use trying to change them. What you can do is impose the rules of Social I.Q. over those of the business meeting, and without actually changing anything that's going on, you can make such gatherings more polite and gracious, and in the process, more efficient—and that means everybody goes to lunch that much earlier.

First, keep in mind that the purpose of a business meeting is to conduct business. It is not to socialize with coworkers or make fun of the boss behind his back, no matter how much fun that might seem at the time. It's not to flirt with the director of public relations or gossip about the torrid affair between the vice president of human resources and the manager of the physical plant. All those things may be going on, but they have to be kept in the background, and they can't ever interfere with the agenda that the supervisors think the meeting is really about.

Second, and most desperately important, is to be on time. Showing up late for a business meeting—or any other kind of meeting—is a terrible way to make an impression. You are demonstrating your lack of compassion for everyone else who bothered to make it on time and are now wasting their precious time waiting for you, and in a more etiquette-book mode, you are simply being rude. There's no excuse for showing up late. Don't do it. It's like neglecting to return a telephone call—a simple thing to do, yet you've chosen to forsake it because it doesn't fit into your schedule. That's rude. You can't do it. Being late is the same thing.

There isn't just one kind of business meeting, either; there are countless types. Some involve groups of people from the same company, planning strategy; others are smaller meetings of committees or groups within the larger office. Some meetings are held between businesspeople and their clients or customers. Other meetings are held to try and convince someone to *become* a client or customer. All have to be treated seriously, and with respect.

Sales meetings. When someone from a company (or someone who *is* the company) meets with a prospective client, both have an agenda. The salesperson (whoever is trying to sell the client on the product or service offered) obviously wants to have the client buy from his or her company. The client wants to get the best product or service at the best price. They don't have to be at odds with each other, but in most cases, both parties are wary of doing the wrong thing.

This is not a book about business, it's about manners, but manners are a very serious issue in this kind of sales meeting. When you're trying to convince someone of something—*anything*—you have to be on your best behavior. In this case it's helpful to remember the Tiffany Theory especially if you know your presentation has weak spots that the client will notice. You present those wrapped in Tiffany paper—with the attractive aspects at the beginning and the end—and don't lie about them.

Still, manners in business go beyond simply saying the right thing the right way. Where will the meeting take place? Often, small meetings, like one-on-one sales pitches, occur over a meal at a restaurant. Traditionally, the person trying to sell will pay the check. But for very small businesses, a very expensive restaurant will be a serious drain on the monthly budget. It is acceptable for the salesperson to let the client choose the restaurant, except when budget is going to be a problem. In that case, it's usually best to suggest a venue or two in a price range acceptable to the person who will be paying. The client can then choose from the suggested choices.

Committee meetings. Small group meetings of people from within the same company are also often held in restaurants, but they are usually much less formal. The bill is generally split among the employees attending, unless the owner of the company is there and wants to pick up the check for his employees.

Committee meetings are sometimes held in the office. While the rules are much less rigidly set than those for larger corporate meetings, they still exist, and some awkward situations can present themselves when the rules aren't as clearly drawn.

For example, it's important to remember the corporate structure even when an informal group is meeting to plan strategy. Just because the executive vice president has rolled up his sleeves and taken off his jacket, it doesn't mean it's acceptable to call him Bob if you've always called him Mr. Henderson. But if you've always been encouraged to use first names with the executives, Bob is perfectly all right. Each situation will be different, and you have to know the rules for your own company.

It's bad manners not to be prepared when you attend a meeting. If you're supposed to have certain materials, you must have them. If you were assigned phone calls to make before the meeting, you must make them before you walk into the conference room. Common sense should prevail, even in a committee meeting.

Large corporate meetings. Annual retreats, large strategy meetings, and other gatherings of departments within large companies have their own structure of etiquette. These rules will vary within companies, but generally speaking, good manners are universal in life. Rude language is unacceptable at all times.

Try not to impose on anyone physically. Shaking hands is usually expected at business meetings, but an arm around a shoulder—particularly between people of opposite sexes—can be seen as going too far. These days, some people are particularly sensitive to sexual harassment, especially in the office, and while there is often no intention to commit such an offense, it's never good manners to "violate someone's personal space," as they used to say in the seventies.

Business meetings are like life, only usually more boring. The same rules apply: if you're called upon to speak, do so in appropriate language and tone. Be prepared. Don't waste everyone's time with jokes, but keep a sense of humor about yourself. Try to make the meeting as pleasant an experience for everyone as you can, but don't go so far as to prepare witty sayings ahead of time. They generally aren't that witty anyway.

Whatever you do, don't attend a horse-designing committee meeting with a plan to add a hump in the back. It's been done.

WHEN BUSINESS AND PLEASURE MIX

I should be sittin' in an air conditioned office in a swivel chair/Talking some trash to the secretary, sayin', "there now, Mama, come on over here."

—JIM CROCE, from the lyrics to
"Workin' at the Car Wash Blues"

It should be noted that behavior described in those lyrics is not an acceptable approach to dating a coworker. In fact, in today's environment (the song was written in the early 1970s, and was tongue-in-cheek even then), it would—and rightly—be considered a form of sexual harassment.

Still, coworkers often date each other, and they quite often form real romances, sometimes marrying. That has happened and will continue to happen for as long as people work together. There is no stopping it, and companies which try, with stated policies against such liaisons, fail more often than not in their attempts to stem the tide.

It makes sense for people who work together to date each other. For one thing, they are the people with whom you share most of your day. It's easiest to start relationships, and get to know people, when you spend a lot of time with them, and work is the place where you're likely to see people with interests and goals similar to your own. Sparks will fly on occasion.

Rather than try and avoid the inevitable, companies are starting to acknowledge, if not encourage, relationships among employees. But the rules of dating in the workplace can be dicey; where business and social worlds collide is a place fraught with danger. Sexual harassment charges are just the beginning. There can be professional blackmail in exchange for a date, the constant wondering if someone is truly interested or merely trying to advance a career, and other doubts about a process that in the real world would be as simple as, "Are you busy Friday night?" and, "Sorry, I have plans."

Let's see how social relationships at work break down and look at each one.

Friendships Among Coworkers

It's easy to make friends at work, particularly when the other employees are at roughly the same level as you are, and their interests are likely to be similar to yours. Problems arise when friendships start to venture outside the office and into personal, but not necessarily sexual, territory.

For example, some employees want their work friends to stay just that—*work* friends. They don't give out their home phone numbers and addresses, and keep their families separate from their professional relationships.

It's difficult and painful for some people to realize that their friends are drawing such boundaries, but they have to be respected. If someone wants to be friendly at work but not outside the office, you can't force them to be.

Friendships Between Management and Employees

This is a very tricky area, and one in which the Social I.Q. of both the employer and the employee can be put to the test. If, for example, your supervisor strikes up a personal conversation, it may be hard for you to explain that you keep your private life private. After all, offending the boss is never a good idea and rarely helps your career.

On the other hand, the employer who is simply making polite conversation can often be seen as too friendly with employees and can be accused of favoritism or worse. Everyone needs to be sensitive to these concerns and take steps to avoid giving the wrong impression. For example:

- Don't gossip about people you see chatting. Gossip is the height of incivility in any situation, but it is worse when people's careers can be damaged.
- As a manager, don't try to insinuate yourself into a group of employees going out for lunch, for example, unless you're invited. Sometimes employees can be a little irre-

verent about management in private, and you don't need to stifle that outlet with your presence.

- As an employee, try to remember that managers are people too. Not every supervisor is trying to intimidate you into being his friend. Caution is commendable; paranoia is not.
- Above all, respect everyone else's boundaries, and stick up for your own as well.

Dating Relationships Among Coworkers

Everything is complicated by romance, or its possibility. It's possible that working relationships are the most complicated of all, since there is no aspect of life quite as public as work or as private as romance. Mix them together, and usually what you get is a serious headache and more gossip than Liz Smith hears in a year.

Here are some quick rules for dating a co-worker on roughly the same professional level as you:

1. Discretion is the better part of survival. Keep it to yourselves.
2. Keep in mind that most dating relationships end. If this is going to be a problem on the job, stop before you start.
3. Early-on in relationships, couples tend to be all over each other. That's cute when you're on your own, but if you do it at the office, the best you can hope for is being talked about; the worst is being fired.
4. Spicy E-mail, photo-copying pictures of body parts, and suggestive Post-It notes are really bad ideas. *Really* bad.
5. See Rule No. 1.

Dating Relationships Between Managers and Employees

When management asks for the date. Managers have more responsibility than employees; that's why they're managers. Managers also have *authority* over employees, and if they don't keep that in mind they can cause enormous problems.

It is almost always more trouble than it's worth for a manager to ask an employee in a lower position out on a date. For one thing, the invitation is bound to be misconstrued, for another, it's very, very difficult for the employee to turn down a supervisor. What happens next year when salary-review time comes around?

Now, having established that this is a bad idea, let's acknowledge that it happens. Given that, what Social I.Q. methods can you use to minimize the chance of damage?

Choose well; don't ask out an employee based strictly on looks if the personality involved is not one suited for such a relationship.

Make absolutely sure the employee understands that she is free to refuse with no threat to her future employment or any other job consideration.

Remember the Ambassador Theory; you are representing not just your gender here, but the company, too. If you do anything out of line, you can be sure your employer will be happy to terminate your employment to save the company serious embarrassment.

Keep in mind you are a teacher, healer, and minister. You can teach your employee that managers are people too; you can heal any misunderstanding with clear information and you can minister to yourself and your employee by being willing to listen.

And finally, you may still want to rethink the whole thing.

If you are an employee being asked out by a supervisor, you're in a sticky situation, indeed. Remember, you have the right to say no, but the die is already cast and you're going to be thinking of this individual differently from now on. Try to separate the person from the job if possible, and make a decision based on what you really want, not what you think you should do for your career.

If you decide to decline, there are ways of doing so that are more polite than others. Say you make it a policy not to date coworkers, but be prepared to back that up if you're asked out by another coworker whom you might actually like to date, since the boss will hear about it. (There are no secrets in the workplace; people only like to think there are.) Say you're seeing someone else, but don't make a point of asking around the office if anyone knows any single people for you to date afterward.

Perhaps honesty is, in fact, the best policy, tell the boss you're not interested, perhaps because it *is* the boss asking. You're entirely within your rights, but try not to be harsh about it. Use the Tiffany Theory when you're forming your response.

If you're the employer being turned down you have one option, and only one: accept no for an answer, walk away, and never do anything that could be construed as retribution for as long as this person is working for or with you. Anything else will be grounds for a lawsuit—the ultimate incivility.

When the employee asks for the date. This is an admittedly less common situation. Employees are usually intimidated by those above them on the corporate ladder, but it occasionally happens that one will ask an employer out. Here the key thing is to realize that rejection doesn't mean anything to your job; it may simply mean that this person isn't interested in you socially or is uncomfortable with such relationships (for all the reasons listed above).

If the manager does agree to the date, things will not get any easier. You asked him out, but as the person with the higher income, should he pay? Actually, no. You initiated the contact and you should pay the tab for the first date. So make sure you propose an event that you can afford.

Breakups

Romance is rarely as easy as it is in the movies. Couples don't always go walking off into the sunset arm-in-arm or ride off together in a limo like Richard Gere and Julia Roberts in *Pretty Woman*. But then hookers rarely look like Julia Roberts and, to be fair, executives don't often look like Richard Gere.

More times than not (a *lot* more), a dating relationship will end badly. That's hard enough to deal with when it's strictly a social situation (we'll get to that shortly), but it's complicated enormously by a dating relationship between coworkers.

Think about it—you just broke up with the person and you have to see him *every day.* That prospect alone should be enough to discourage you from an office romance, but in case it's not, try to remember a few Social I.Q. pointers for the semi-inevitable:

1. You can't let your anger or disappointment affect your work.
2. You have to treat your ex as if she were just another colleague.
3. Be polite.
4. Be efficient in your work.
5. If your ex is your boss, it might be best to look for a new job, and don't say we didn't warn you.
6. Remember the rule about discretion. Everyone, even your ex, deserves to be treated politely.
7. If he's not treating you politely, take the high road. Otherwise you're sure to end up watching your professional performance plummet. Read Rule 1 again.

Marriages Within a Company

Those few relationships that can navigate the corporate waters can lead to marriages between coworkers. If you're invited to the wedding, keep in mind that these people are your coworkers and try to attend. Bring a gift. You don't have to get a better gift because the bride or the groom is your supervisor.

A wedding is a social event. If you are marrying a coworker and inviting coworkers, expect office politics to play a role. Try as hard as you can not to bring the pressures of the wedding to the office, and don't hold a grudge against coworkers who can't attend or who bring an inexpensive gift.

The key to all office relationships is to keep it out of the office.

Now, if you think *that* was complicated, you're ready to discuss dating in the modern age.

Keep in Mind

- All people in business are entitled to courtesy.
- Business meetings are for business, not socializing.
- Defer to a supervisor when necessary, and correct or question them privately, later.
- Dating coworkers should keep in mind that romantic relationships can't ever impact on the office.
- A little discretion never hurts. A lot of discretion is even better.

THE OFFICE QUIZ

Five points for a right answer; no fair peeking at the answers. Add the points up at the end. Good luck.

1. Technology is the enemy of:
   a. civility.
   b. reverence.
   c. science
   d. T.H.R.U.S.H.

Answer: B. Technology has taken over communication, and in doing so, is battling the idea of reverence, of respect for others. Give yourself two points if you answered A., though, since civility is a casualty of the war.

2. The purpose of a business meeting is to:
   a. promote sales.
   b. get to know the staff better.
   c. conduct business.
   d. all of the above

Answer: C. While the other things can happen at a business meeting, it is important to remember that the idea here is to conduct business, and not to work toward your own personal agenda, flirt or make friends.

3. When attending a business meeting, it is essential to:
   a. dress nicely.
   b. prepare ahead of time.
   c. show up on time.
   d. all of the above

Answer: D. Okay, so there are business meetings that won't require you to dress well, but you should anyway. Remember, you're an ambassador. And preparation, not to mention punctuality, are absolutely imperative.

4. When a sales meeting takes place at a restaurant:
   a. the person selling pays the check
   b. the person buying pays the check.
   c. the check is split.
   d. the person with the higher salary pays the check.

Answer: A. You're asking someone to spend money on your company. Asking him to spend money on your lunch while you try to convince him to spend more on your product or service isn't just rude; it's bad business.

5. When two people working together begin a romantic relationship, gossip is:
   a. rude.
   b. an intrusion of privacy.
   c. inevitable.
   d. all of the above

Answer: D. It's horrible, it's unfair, it's absolutely unacceptable, and you'd better get used to it, because you will be the subject of office gossip if you start dating a co-worker. And be ready for 90 percent of what's said about you to be untrue.

6. The Cardinal Rule of office romance is:
   a. no sex in the copy room.
   b. keep the relationship separate from work.
   c. don't ask out a subordinate.
   d. all of the above

Answer: B. Not that you *should* have sex in the copy room, but it's most important to remember that our performance at work should remain consistent no matter what is going on in your personal life. Kissy noises across the room or angry glares during a personal argument are enough to get you fired. Don't start down that road.

7. When a supervisor is asking an employee out on a date, it's important to make clear that:
   a.   sex on the first date is not expected.
   b.   neither party is married.
   c.   no professional consequences will come from an answer of "no."
   d.   all of the above

Answer: C. In today's climate of sexual harassment lawsuits, make it absolutely clear that no consequences, positive or negative, are part of this request. This is one person asking another out; the professional part of the relationship is entirely separate.

8. Business meetings can never be hurt with the injection of a little humor. True or false?

Answer: False. While humor is not the worst thing that could happen to most business meetings, it's important to remember that this occasion is not a performance of stand-up comedy. Don't prepare jokes (unless you're being called upon to address a large group with a written text) and don't push the limits. If you're not funny, acknowledge that and move on.

9. When a supervisor and an employee do go out on a date:
   a.   the boss always pays.
   b.   the employee always pays.
   c.   the person who did the inviting should pay.
   d.   the check should be split.

Answer: C. No matter who did the asking, that person has requested the pleasure of another's company. For that pleasure, one should be prepared to pay the check. If the person with the lower salary is inviting, the person being asked should expect to be treated to something affordable.

10. When an inter-office romance breaks up:
   a.   one employee or the other should request a transfer to another department.

b. one employee or the other should request a transfer to another *facility*.
c. it's important to act as if nothing has changed.
d. none of the above

Answer: C. Under the best circumstances, fellow employees shouldn't even be aware the romance is over until you tell them. Acrimony, revenge and backbiting are all bad ideas in any event, and worse buy a factor of 1,000 in the office.

Score

0–10: You're unemployed, aren't you?
11–20: Bottom of the promotion list.
21–30: Work harder; you'll get the gold watch.
31–40: Management training program.
41–50: Congrats! You got that raise!

3

Dating

DATING 101

Dating isn't what it used to be, but then, maybe it never was.

—SYDNEY BIDDLE BARROWS AND ELLIS WEINER,
Mayflower Manners

Few things are as confusing as dating. Part mating ritual, part audition process, it encompasses virtually every question and problem involved in the Social I.Q., and blends them, combines them, twisting them into something that is completely unique. It's amazing anyone manages to get anything right when they're dating. It is the center of the awkward situation universe.

Beginning with the decision to ask someone out, dating is infinitely more complicated than it was thirty years ago. Some women are comfortable asking a man on a date; others aren't. By the same token, some men have no problem with a woman asking them out, while others consider it unthinkable. The bottom line: if you think it's all right and the other person doesn't, you have already identified an area in which you are not compatible.

Even from that moment, however, there is no relief from the number of awkward situations dating offers, and the sexes have no end to their complaints about each other's behavior in the dating arena. Women say men are inconsiderate, don't call when they say they will, don't listen when they talk, and spend all their time trying to maneuver them into bed. Men say women see them as walking ATM machines, wanting to be taken to expensive restaurants and pricey events, and bought expensive gifts, but are rarely even grateful when those things are presented.

Who's right? It doesn't really matter. Perception is enough, and it creates tension between the genders that makes the purpose of dating—finding a mate, enjoying someone's company, and establishing a relationship—all the more clouded and pushed into the background. If you're busy worrying about the details, you might lose sight of the prize itself. So keep your eyes on the prize. The details? I'm about to settle those for you.

Some people are perfectly happy dating more than one person at a time, while others are "serial monogamists," unable to start a new relationship while another is ongoing. Again, neither of these positions is wrong, but be forewarned: the minute one relationship gets serious—that is, when it's no longer just dating but becomes a "relationship," the other one must be ended. It is profoundly inconsiderate to both people you're dating to continue once one relationship has begun to flower.

Never, *ever* keep one relationship secret. It requires lying, which is always unacceptable, and deceit, which is not even worth discussing in a book on treating people well. It is an insult to both people you're dating, and a sign that you're not truly interested in seeing any of these relationships take flight (if you have three or more relationships going a the same time, you must be exhausted!). Casual dating is a fine thing, but it has to be the goal of both people in the relationship. If one is after a quick fling and the other is thinking in longer terms, trouble will erupt. Communicate your intentions as you go, and make sure both people in each relationship understand what they want. If it's not the same thing, it's time to stop seeing each other.

Just remember: each person you're about to ask out (or hope will ask you out) is different. And each reaction to each situation will be different, and unpredictable. Dating, remember, is the most complicated of all awkward situations. In fact, it is a compilation of awkward situations, all coming together at once. Think of dating as Social I.Q.'s Greatest Hits. Ready? Let's go on a date (but don't expect me to pick up the check).

DATING IN THE NEW MILLENNIUM, OR WHY OLD RULES ARE GOOD RULES

The difficulty with marriage is that we fall in love with a personality, but must live with a character.

—Peter DeVries

Everyone agrees that dating used to be easier, but it was never easy. Thirty or forty years ago the rules of dating etiquette were much clearer, and everybody knew them. The man asked the woman out; the man paid the bill; sex came after marriage. Okay, maybe fifty years ago for the last one.

The difference now is that the rules haven't just changed; they've been obliterated. For men, confusion rules the day. If you ask a woman to dinner, does that mean you're paying the check? For a woman, if you ask a man to dinner, does that mean you're forward and threatening?

Awkward situation: you're a woman, and you find a man attractive and interesting. You gather up your nerve and call him to ask him to dinner, but he gives you a quick excuse and declines. Later on, you hear through a mutual friend that he thought your asking him out was a signal that you didn't respect him and were desperate for a date. If you had waited, he tells your friend, he would have asked you out.

Did you do something wrong? Well, yes and no. No, you didn't break any established rules of etiquette, since it has been perfectly acceptable for some time for a woman to invite a man to dinner. Yes, clearly you made a mistake, because the man you asked was offended. Either you shouldn't ask anymore, or you simply asked the wrong man. At the earliest possible point, your personality and his did not click. That's a major warning.

Awkward situation: you're a man and you see a woman quite often at a health club. She's a member, and you come to play racquetball with your considerably more upscale friend. She is clearly more affluent than you are. You want to ask her out, but she's obviously used to the better things and you can't afford them. What to do?

Let's examine the options. You can assume she'll say no to a movie and a dinner, and you save up for weeks to take her out on one date, which you consider a romantic gesture. Or, you could assume she'll say no to a blue-collar guy like yourself, and give up entirely before you start. Or, you can come clean, tell her you're dying to ask her out but can't afford to spend a week's salary on an evening, and propose a less expensive date.

How well does each of these tactics work? Well, giving up before you start never does anybody any good, so that one's out altogether. If you're interested in someone, you should ask her out. It's like your mother always told you: "The worst that can happen is that she'll say no."

Saving up for a month in order to pay for one night is a grand gesture, all right, but it might give off the wrong signal: that you can, in fact, afford the extravagance you've decided this woman is accustomed to. You'd be starting the relationship off on a misconception, and that's not a very healthy sign. Strike two.

The best course of action is to own up. For one thing, the woman might not be a member of the health club, just like you, and might not be accustomed to pricey restaurants and extravagant evenings. Or, she might be exactly as you've imagined, but she might not care that you don't make a huge salary. The fact is, if she's interested in seeing you, she'll either accept your low-rent invitation, or she'll offer to split the evening. In either case, you'll know she's interested.

These two examples, though, illustrate exactly how convoluted and confusing the dating scene has become as we approach the end of the millennium. The intricacies of dating have become so subtle and so minute as to be almost impossible to see in some cases, yet they can make the difference between happily establishing a meaningful relationship and spending another Saturday night with your Blockbuster membership card. Let's get specific.

WHO CALLS WHOM?

Don't call us; we'll call you.

—Everyone in Hollywood

You want a nice, clean, easy answer, don't you? I can tell. Up to this point, you've only been reading so you can find out: Who's supposed to call and make the invitation for the first date? I'm sorry to disappoint you. There's no simple answer.

Let's get one thing clear right away: it is perfectly acceptable for a woman to call a man and ask him out. I know I've said it before, but it needs to be clear. There's absolutely no breach of etiquette in that action. The problem is, some men aren't going to like it.

To be perfectly honest, part of the problem is that women don't like making that first phone call any more than men ever did. It's a hideous experience—nervousness, emotional vulnerability, leaving yourself open for rejection that can't be disguised. Who would *want* to do that?

But women fought hard to be treated equally, both professionally and personally, and, alas, the first-date call was part of the deal. Granted, we men put it in the fine print so you wouldn't notice it right away, but it's there, and women are stuck with it, just the way men have been stuck with it since the invention of the telephone.

Amazingly, though, some men don't want to relinquish the right to make fools of themselves. They feel there's something unseemly in a woman calling and asking them out. That makes it all the more difficult for two groups: women who want the freedom to initiate a relationship, and men who don't mind women calling at all and would love to be let off the hook.

Thus the awkward situation: How can a woman tell if a man will be happy she called or put off? The hard answer is: she can't, no more than a man ever could when he called a woman for a first date. You've just got to take a deep breath and dial the number like the rest of us. I'm sorry.

What does etiquette have to say about it? Well, anyone can ask anyone, but there are ways of doing so that are correct and some that are not. The do's and don'ts are the same for men and women:

- Do suggest a specific event.
- Don't just say: "Are you busy Friday night?"
- Do try to include mutual interests: movies, dining—whatever.
- Don't buy the tickets before you ask—that's too much pressure.
- Do answer with a clear yes or no when being asked out.
- Don't ask someone out on voice mail or an answering machine.
- Do plan the evening carefully; don't be inflexible if the person you're asking wants to make a few minor changes.

Think of making that first phone call as a privilege: you get to choose which person you'd like to ask out, what event you'd like to attend, and when you'd like to call and do the asking. They don't. It's an advantage, not a burden. Okay, so it's an advantage that brings with it the cold sweats and stammering that first-date calls always have (even for the smoothest of operators), but it's an advantage nonetheless.

Remember, too, that it's not so easy being the person who gets called. If she says yes, that's a very strong sign. If she says no but sounds regretful, or adds "maybe another time," you have another chance. If she says no and leaves it at that, perhaps you should do the same.

Nobody said this was going to be easy.

FIRST DATES

We're just gonna go home later, right, and there's gonna be all that tension. You know, we never kissed before, and I'll never know when to make the right move or anything. So we'll kiss now, we'll get it over with, and then we'll go eat.

—WOODY ALLEN as Alvy Singer, in *Annie Hall*

Just the idea of a first date is enough to send otherwise strong adults into a cold sweat. On the surface, there's nothing scary about a first date, unless one happens to be going out with Norman Bates. The only danger involved is emotional, and tenuous at that. The worst thing that can happen to you is that someone you don't know (in almost all cases) will turn out not to be your soul mate. That's the worst thing.

Of course, deep down, everybody knows that—but it doesn't stop the cold sweats at all.

First dates are meant to be several things: part social occasion, part job interview. First dates are opportunities to get to know another person, possibilities for meeting the love of your life, and/or chances to find someone with whom to have sex. They can be nerve-wracking, uncomfortable, disastrous, or scary. What most people forget is that they're also supposed to be *fun*.

Yes, fun. The whole idea of a date is to get together for an event. Now, the event might be something as simple as lunch together, or it could involve tickets to the symphony, a hansom cab ride around the park and dinner in a rooftop restaurant. But the key idea is that the event is central to the date.

If either of the people involved isn't interested in the event being suggested ("I don't care for ballet," "Well, I *hate* hockey"), the person doing the suggesting should have a backup event ready, hopefully one that will be more acceptable to each ("How about a movie?"). If you can't both agree on a movie, perhaps there's a message you're missing here.

What event is attended is not important; what's important is that both people on the date want to be there, because once you've identified a common interest, the event itself should be enjoyable for both parties, and that's where the concept of a *fun* first date comes in.

Here are a few etiquette tips for first dates:

It's still customary for the man to arrive at the woman's home and take her to the event. Some women, however, are more concerned about security, especially when they don't know the man very well and prefer to meet in a public place.

Neither party should spend too much time talking about himself or herself. It's rude and gives the implicit message that you're not interested in the other person, but believe he or she should be interested in you.

Movies, concerts, and other special events are fine, but they don't leave much time for conversation (the real reason you're getting together is to get to know each other). Try to plan a time before or after the event—dinner, dessert, coffee) when you can talk.

It is *not* okay to break the date less than twenty-four hours before you are supposed to meet, especially if it's because someone better has presented an invitation. You made the commitment, now follow up on it.

The day after the first date, either party (ideally, both parties) should call or send a note thanking the other for the lovely time, even if you don't intend to see this person again. A note is better than a phone call. E-mail is better than nothing—but not much.

Forget what you've seen in the movies. It is *not* okay to call your best friend seconds after your date has left and discuss every intimate detail of the evening, especially to giggle over how inept he or she was. Discretion is the better part of valor.

Blind Dates

A certain percentage of the population—a rather large percentage, in fact—meets by plan, even if it isn't their plan. A lot of couples are fixed up by friends, relatives, and even exes, and others use dating services, computer dating, personal ads, and in this day and age, the Internet to meet potential dates. What does this do to the first date?

Well, for one thing, it makes the experience that much more tense. It's one thing to be going out on a date with someone you don't know; it's quite another to date someone you've never seen. Some of dating is physical attraction, and it's hard to know if you have that before you've laid eyes on the person you're dating, not to mention that dating someone you're meeting based on information they have provided to a dating service or in a personal ad puts you at the mercy of someone you've never actually met.

In the case of blind dates, it's usually best to meet in a public place. Make sure you've either given an accurate description of yourself or be sure that you're wearing something (or carrying something) that will identify you to the person you're meeting. Think of the limousine drivers at the airport holding little signs with their clients' names on them; there's nothing easier to spot than your own name. In the case of a blind date, though, a flower in a lapel or even a baseball cap (but specify the team) is enough to make you stand out.

By the way, if you happen to be the "fixer-upper" rather than the "fixed-up," have a little compassion. Just because you've decided that two people are meant for each other doesn't mean *they'll* decide the same thing. If one or the other declines your suggestion, leave it at that. If they do decide to meet, don't be on the phone every half hour trying to get details. You've done your part; now step aside and let your friends carve out their own relationship, or not.

If you're going on a blind date and you're disappointed with the looks of your date when you meet, it is the utmost in impoliteness to let that show. For one thing, you would be insulting someone before you get to know them, and you could be missing the chance to get to know someone with whom you might have a lot in common, even if physical attraction isn't part of it. Go on the date as planned, and you might even have a good time. But don't lie: If you're not interested in a second date, don't pretend that you are.

Other Ways to Meet

Where do you go to meet the right person these days? The short answer: anywhere.

TEN GREAT PLACES TO
MEET POTENTIAL DATES

- The ballpark (I'll bet you thought I was going to say the supermarket)
- The supermarket
- Microbreweries
- Night classes
- Bowling alleys
- Book signings
- Libraries
- The video store
- The beach (or pool, if you have no beach)
- Wine tastings

Personal Ads

Don't scoff. Personal ads are a very valid way to meet someone who might become your significant other. They are also fraught with danger, and have an etiquette all their own.

If you're placing a personal ad, it's important not to lie, because anyone in whom you're interested is going to find out the truth, anyway. But you can present yourself in the most favorable light possible. Have a sense of humor about yourself. If you weigh three hundred pounds and you're under seven feet tall, describe yourself as "dietetically challenged" ("zaftig" has become old hat). But emphasize your warm heart, your fondness for children, and your wry sense of humor.

Do *not* include a photo of yourself, an address, or a phone number. Let the publication in which you're placing the ad supply you with a post office box number. There are too many unbalanced people out there; don't let them know where you live.

If you're responding to a personal ad, once again, honesty is the best policy. Relax if you're responding in writing; loosen up and have some fun with your letter. If you're responding by voice mail, use your real voice; don't try to sound sexy. No two people agree on what that quality might be, anyway. Your best bet—your *only* bet—is to be yourself.

Also, don't you give out your address or phone number. If the publication provides a way of meeting—through the post office box, for example—use it. If not, provide a phone number, but make it your business phone number. You don't want anyone to be able to trace you to your home until you meet and trust that person.

Who Pays?

Feminism be damned; the fact of the matter is, the man is still the one who *usually* pays on a first date (and often on subsequent dates). Note the italics on *usually*. I don't dismiss the number of women who feel it is their right to pick up a check, or at least half of one, but most women one talks to say they want to see the man pay for the first date.

This is part of the same mind-set that still has men calling women the first time for a date. Women want to know that they have the equality feminism tried to get them in the 1970s (and since), but traditionalists still like to be called and have their dates paid for.

But is there a hard-and-fast rule of etiquette on the subject? Not really. The accepted standard is that the person who calls and does the inviting is offering to pay, and therefore should pick up the check. And since men still do the majority of first-date calling, they also do the bulk of first-date paying. Still, if the man is making demonstrably less money than the woman, the woman should at least offer to split the check. If the man invites her to an event she feels is meant to fit a budget and she can afford it, the woman can always suggest an alternative event and offer to pay the difference.

Luckily, one thing feminism did manage to achieve is the prominence of women in the workplace, and most single women work. It helps, because it makes it easier for men and women to discuss money, and the more honest talk there is on a first date (or at any other time), the better. If there's a problem with money, say so. If she doesn't want to go out with you because you don't have enough money, you're better off knowing now that she's shallow and rude.

Sex on the First Date

One thing must be made clear: a man (or, for that matter, a woman) has *absolutely no right* to expect sex in return for a date, first or any thereafter. Picking up a check doesn't entitle you to anything other than polite conversation and the call or note specified earlier. If you expect sex because you've spent money, you should patronize a prostitute.

Now, that said: If a woman has sex with a man on the first date, does that make her a prostitute? Of course not. Sometimes two people are physically drawn together with such great power that it's difficult to wait until after the first date. But they both have to agree that they want sex; it's just silly to hop into bed because "I felt like I owed it to him" or "she seemed to really want to."

Physical attraction is a strange thing; it can't be measured scientifically. Sometimes two people feel it so strongly that sex is virtually a given; other times, people who care about each other deeply simply have no desire for each other physically. And sexual politics has at least progressed to the point that we should recognize exactly *why* we want to sleep with someone. If it's strictly physical and both parties know that, it's okay. If two people come together with different agendas, however, it can cause enormous emotional trouble for both.

For what it's worth, I think sex on the first date is usually a mistake. People who don't really know each other should be careful about how intimate they become quickly. Time won't hurt, and if there's a very strong attraction, you can be reasonably sure there will be a second date.

At this point it should go without saying that if you're having sex with someone for the first time, a condom is absolutely essential. The consequences of not using one can be much, much too serious to do without. For the record: the man should bring birth control with him if he even considers sleeping with this woman, but a smart woman who's dating should have condoms in her bedroom, anyway. Embarrassment just isn't important in the face of AIDS and other sexually transmitted diseases, not to mention unwanted pregnancy. By the way, simply kissing on the first date is between you and your lips. Either decision is okay.

Gifts

It is not too much to want to give someone a gift after a successful first date (and the definition of a successful first date is: "one you enjoyed well enough to want to see this person again," not necessarily "order the invitations"). It isn't essential, but it's not too much.

The key, however, is not going overboard. Sending a woman flowers after a date is nice; sending her a big-screen TV is going too far. Don't send the signal that after one evening you're already too involved in this relationship after one evening, or you will almost certainly scare the other person off.

Don't send a ring from a Cracker Jack box, either, though. Unless it has some humorous resonance between the two of you, it's going to be seen as the ultimate in cheap gestures, and somewhat insulting at that.

Yes, it's okay for a woman to send a man a gift too, and the same rules apply. You *can* send flowers to a man if you think he'll appreciate the gesture.

Always remember: the object of a first date is to clear the path for a second date. And, of course, to have fun.

DATING FOR MEN

I know men. They're basically filthy and nasty and dirty. See, I used to be a man before I got married.

—BILL COSBY

Dating—which we will define here as a relationship that goes on after the first date and lasts until engagement or cohabitation—is a different experience for men than it is for women. Again, we're dealing here in general terms, as there are men and women so well matched that they seem to experience the same things in the same ways, but they are the exception rather than the rule.

For a man, the second date relieves some of the pressure of the first. For one thing, he has had a chance to see and talk to the woman before the date this time, and knows what to expect. He doesn't necessarily have to call and make the invitation for a second date; the woman might, but it's still less likely than the man calling. He may not have to pay the whole bill this time, either.

On dates after the second, a relationship is being formed, and the two people will find their own style. They might alternate calling; they might split the bill. Usually, the rule becomes "whoever invites buys the tickets (or meal)," but whatever works for each couple will take shape in the days, weeks, or months after the first date.

The issue of sex is often seen differently by men and women. Men are often waiting for the opportunity to make love to the woman as soon as possible, if they are attracted to her to begin with. Somewhere along the line, the third date became the line of demarcation: if they make it to a third date, some men expect the woman to sleep with them at that point.

It can't be said enough times: if one person or the other is not interested in having sex, you don't have sex. It doesn't matter how many dates you've gone on. The only other choice for a man (or a woman) who thinks the relationship should take a more physical turn, but whose partner is not ready, is to end the relationship. Don't threaten to end the relationship as a form of sexual blackmail. Discuss the situation; find out if the woman's (in most cases) decision not to have sex now is based on a general one she's made about sex, or if it has to do with you. Also find out in very general terms how long (or to what point) she thinks you should wait, and if that's not acceptable to you, you can either wait until she's ready or determine that the relationship isn't going to work out and end it.

Keep in Mind

- Show interest: flowers, cards, notes, and phone calls are welcome.
- Never, *ever* promise to call a woman and then don't do so.
- Listen to what she says, and stop talking long enough to let her say it.
- It is rude to avoid eye contact in a restaurant because you're watching sports on the overhead TV. Get the score later on ESPN, after you return home. Now, look at your date.
- After the second date, cook dinner for her once in a while.

DATING FOR WOMEN

Romance, Stone, is the only thing we can be sure all women want.

—PETER O'TOOLE as Alan Swann, in *My Favorite Year*

Let's get one thing straight, right away: it is desperately important to most women that the phone ring the day after a first date, and it had better be the man they dated on the other end of the line.

Women, first of all, want to know that there is something to a man's interest other than simple physical attraction. They have usually dated enough men with "just one thing on their minds" to be suspicious, and the fact that a man has the consideration to call the next day, or send a note (which takes a little longer, but is a more romantic gesture), is important. Some men feel silly doing things like that, but they shouldn't. There's nothing wrong with making someone feel special.

Beyond that, dating for women is a process that feels like a constant pop quiz: measure up and the man will continue to call; give a wrong answer and you'll find yourself cut off without an explanation. It's no wonder women view the whole dating process with some measure of distrust.

The flip side, of course, is that men are often just as off-balance during dating. Women need to know that men are less likely to pick up the signals that women send out; when a woman tells a man that he can't come into her apartment after a date because she has to get up early for work, she may very well be indicating that she's not ready to sleep with him yet. The man, however, may take her at her word, and not get the message.

Communication is the key to all relationships, not just romantic ones. The key to Social I.Q. is to present the truth in as polite and positive a fashion as possible. Women can certainly tell a man they're not ready for intimacy yet, but they should keep their ambassador role in perspective—it's not necessary to have sex with a man to be polite; it *is* necessary to explain to him why you're not ready (or just not interested.) to do so with him.

- No matter what you've heard, sex is not all there is to dating, even for men.
- Don't assume the man you're dating this time is just like the last man you dated. A lot of really nice men are tired of paying the price for the boors who came before them.
- A man is not an ATM machine. You don't have to pay for things (unless you've mutually agreed or you're making a lot more money than he is), but you do, definitely, have to show gratitude for gifts and gestures. (That goes for both men and women.)
- You don't have to take care of a man; he's not a child. Don't stay in a relationship because "he needs me." Stay in a relationship because you want to.
- Men have feelings, too. Let him talk about them sometimes.
- Send a note or call after a date. You don't have to wait for the phone to ring; this isn't the fifties.

DATING FOR DIVORCED OR RECENTLY SEPARATED SINGLES

"What do you mean, I don't believe in marriage? I've been married twice." "See what I mean?"

—CARY GRANT as Roger O. Thornhill and EVA MARIE SAINT as Eve Kendall, in *North by Northwest*

Every awkward situation is different, but for people reentering the dating world after a long-term relationship, *awkward* is barely an adequate word. Try *excruciating*.

A first date will be difficult for both people, not just the one

recently uncoupled. The person who just ended a long relationship will usually have negative memories of the previous
partner, and the new person on the scene will wonder what
went wrong, whose fault it was, and whether it's possible to
measure up or repair the damage. Six bellboys couldn't carry all
the baggage that's being lugged around here.

DATING SOMEONE NEWLY
AVAILABLE AGAIN

Consideration goes beyond the usual rules of etiquette here. It's
important to tread lightly near a recent divorcee, widow, or
someone who has simply ended a long relationship. Most likely
you will find exposed emotional nerves. A little understanding
is likely to go a long way. The roles of teacher and minister here
might take a back seat to the role of healer, since there is much
damage that needs to be repaired, even in the most amicable of
separations.

Remember the healing role: empathy is key. If you have been
through a similar experience, you can understand what needs to
be done. If you haven't, you can imagine. In any event, you can
certainly take steps to begin the healing process.

You also have to remember that this might not be your
lifelong companion; some people really do need that transitional
relationship, and you might have just come along at the wrong
time. It's important to go into a relationship like this with both
eyes open; even if you don't end up spending your life with this
person, you can still help heal, and do so without sacrificing
your dignity or your romantic dreams. It just takes a little
empathy, and a lot of consideration. Expect unpredictable
emotions; remember, there are raw nerves at work here.

Be at your highest level of Social I.Q.: overlook some things
you might not in other situations, but not to the point of
becoming a doormat.

Try as hard as you can to not even think about the person who came before you. Madness lies that way, whether your predecessor was a sinner or a saint.

The person in whom you're interested may be reluctant to show affection in public, or even to introduce you as anything other than "my friend." You have to take this in stride.

The first sexual encounter might be later in the relationship than you'd normally expect; this person has been burned badly and you can't see when the bandages come off. Be understanding.

You're Dating Again

For the person whose relationship has just ended—by divorce, death, or mutual agreement—dating raises a host of questions, many of which are difficult and sometimes painful to answer. It's easier to ignore them, and more comfortable.

Still, at some point you're going to be ready to start a new relationship. Trust me, you will, so you might as well know the answers to some of those difficult questions now.

First, the answer to most questions about when something is appropriate is: when you feel ready. That applies to taking off a wedding ring, if that is an issue. It applies to when it's proper to date again (although a couple of weeks after a spouse dies is in awful taste). And it applies to when you're ready to have sex with someone new. It may apply as well to things like photographs of your ex that might be displayed (or not) around your home.

Once these questions are answered—again, all with the somewhat complicated response "when you feel ready"—it's time to start considering what you're looking for in a new relationship. Is this going to be a "rebound" situation, or a transitional relationship? Do you have no intention of starting another serious relationship right away? It's fine to have those feelings, but as soon as it seems appropriate to discuss such things, it's necessary to let your date know what your intentions are. It's not fair to let someone new believe you might be interested in starting a life together if all you're doing is testing the dating waters after a long time away.

Remember that communication is key. The more you can discuss with your new partner, the better a chance you have of creating a satisfying new relationship, or surviving the new dating experience without any more serious emotional scars.

A Few Awkward Situations

You're out on your first date since the divorce, and you run into your ex-brother-in-law (or, worse, your ex-mother-in-law). You can act guilty and detach yourself from your date ("This is my friend, Bob.") or greet your ex-in-law warmly and make it clear you're dating again.

There's no easy answer. Each divorce is different, and your relationship with your ex-in-law might be amicable or not-so-amicable, so you have to gauge your own feelings. One thing is certain: it is cold and rude to deny that you're dating someone who is standing next to you. The truth shall set you free. Or at least give you a better chance for a second date.

You were married for fifteen years before your husband passed away. Now, a year after his death, you're dating again, and the man you've dated twice expects you to sleep with him.

It doesn't matter if things are different now than they used to be. Pressure is pressure, and it is always unacceptable. If you want to make love with the man, go ahead. If you don't, make sure you don't, and tell him in no uncertain terms that you're not ready and you don't appreciate the pressure.

Your friend just broke up with his girlfriend after eight years together, and he's depressed. You want to fix him up with a woman from your office, but he says that he's not interested in dating yet.

It is absolutely wrong for you to argue that "you weren't married, or anything." A long-term relationship, with or without a marriage license, is a very painful thing to dissolve, and as a healer and a minister your job is to listen, not to argue. Some people do need a nudge to start dating after a serious relationship breaks up, but you have to have some compassion, too. Don't joke about it, and don't be glib. Put your matchmaking plans on hold until your friend says he's ready.

DATING FOR SINGLE PARENTS

I married your mother because I wanted children.
Imagine my disappointment when you arrived.

> —GROUCHO MARX, as Professor Quincy Adams Wagstaff,
> to ZEPPO MARX, as Frank Wagstaff, in *Horsefeathers*
> written by Bert Kalmar and Harry Ruby.

Children change everything. Let me say that again: children change everything. For single parents, dating is all the same tension, pain, and worry that it is for people without children, but there's another layer of anxiety on top of that. The responsibility for a child makes romantic leaps of faith all the more difficult. A wrong choice can damage more than just your own life.

There are few desires stronger in humans than the one to make one's children happy. After divorce, especially, when the ex-spouse is still around and (to the child's mind) available, dating represents a threat that the ideal arrangement—Mom and Dad together again—will never come true. Forget that the adults have already decided that; children believe in happy endings.

Of course, this situation creates tension for all parties involved: for the newly single person considering dating again, for the person entering the situation as a possible new spouse, and for the child. Add in the ex-spouse, who often will be involved in child care in one way or another, and assorted friends and relatives, and you have complications the Brady Bunch never dreamed of.

THE SINGLE PARENT

Bringing a new romance into a home with a child can produce more guilt faster than Nancy Walker could as the stereotypical Jewish mother on *Rhoda*. The single parent often feels guilty simply for having feelings of desire that are all hers; she'll quite often deny her own needs in the mistaken belief that her child will benefit.

The truth is, making yourself miserable is likely to do the same to your child. Kids pick up the feelings in their home; remember, the toxic effects of bad feelings are just as damaging as the physical effects of secondhand smoke or holes in the ozone layer. You're doing harm to your child if you suppress yourself in your child's name. Whether you admit it or not, you'll end up resenting the child, and he'll know it.

Does that mean you should ignore your child's feelings and do whatever you want? Of course not. Have some discretion. Do not, under any circumstances, bring a date home until you're sure (a) that your child can handle the idea, and (b) that the person you're dating is going to last past two or three dates. Children, especially the children of divorce, need stability. You can have your affairs, but keep them out of your child's life until they become significant parts of your own.

The Date

If you are becoming involved with someone who has children, it is not your responsibility to be the child's parent. If you marry, you will become the stepparent, but until that step is at least being contemplated, you are simply a friend of the child's parent.

Your responsibility is filled with *nots*: you are *not* supposed to replace the ex-spouse as a parent. You are *not* in competition with the child for the parent's affections. You are *not* supposed to discipline the child if the parent is in the same room, and not even in the same house, unless the parent has clearly left you in charge.

You are also not there to make comparisons. Children will often try to get what they want by playing one adult against another: "You know, Dad never let me do that when I wanted to." Your desire to be liked by the child, as well as the parent you're dating, may lead to an impulse to indulge every whim of the child, buy elaborate gifts or take them on too-frequent outings. You are not a fantasy parent, either.

For the most part, you should take your lead from the adult you're dating. If he asks you to watch his child for a while so he can go to the supermarket and you feel comfortable with that, go ahead. But if you don't feel free to discuss your feelings about this, you may not be dating the right person.

What if you don't like the person's child? That's an awkward situation of titanic proportions. You have to weigh your feelings for the parent very carefully. After all, the parent's responsibility and allegiance should go to the child, so if you truly can't live in the child's presence, you have serious problems in your relationship.

Now, the ex-spouse. Jealousy is bound to rampant on both sides of that fence. Remember that this person is also the child's parent, and you're not. Defer, even when you think the ex is wrong, unless you're clearly seeing physical abuse of the child. Otherwise you're an observer. Until you marry into the family, you're a guest here.

The Ex

It's very easy to see the ex-spouse of a divorced parent as Captain Hook. Whatever the circumstances of the divorce or separation, if your ex starts to date again, you are going to be seen as a threat by the new companion, an impediment by your ex-spouse, and an alternative by your child. It's not easy filling any of those roles, even if none of them is your intention.

Don't reject your ex's new lover simply on the grounds that he's not you. It is, in fact, none of your business if your ex is dating, and if so, whom she's dating. The only time you can step into the situation is when you see evidence that your child is being abused, and at that moment, you should act quickly.

Expect pressure from your child, who is being wooed, in a

sense, by the new companion. Remember that no matter what happens, you're still the parent. You will be if your ex remarries or if he or she doesn't. You get to be the parent for the rest of your life, no matter what. For a lot of people, that's enough.

WHEN LOVE ENDS

What do you do when the love that you feel/Turns out to be one dream that never came true?
>   —GERRY RAFFERTY, from the lyrics to "Hang On"

You thought I was going to quote "Breaking Up Is Hard to Do," by Neil Sedaka, didn't you?

I know a man who was involved in a long-term relationship with a woman who had a child. He had become close to both of them, and one day she ended the relationship. On the phone.

You're groaning, aren't you? Everyone does when they hear that story. It is a perfect example of the decline of manners and consideration in our society. I suppose it could have been worse. She could have broken up with his answering machine.

Something like that incident goes beyond awkward. It is classless and unforgivable, and illustrates exactly why technology is the enemy of reverence. If your relationship has to end, it has to end, but if you have any manners at all, it has to end face-to-face. Using a telephone, an answering machine, voice mail, E-mail or any other substitute for a personal encounter is absolutely unacceptable. This is one example in which even a handwritten note is not good enough.

That is not to say that ending a relationship is ever easy. I can understand why someone would want to avoid having to look into another person's face while they lower the boom, but sometimes we have to forget our own concerns and just do what's right. There is no way to break up a relationship other than in person.

Why is it so hard to end a romance? Well, think about it: here's someone in whom you had at least enough interest to go out with on a number of dates (a one-night stand does not qualify here), someone you were considering, at least for a time, as a potential mate, someone whose feelings you have cared about. Deliberately hurting that person is never going to be easy. There has to be a right way to do it.

And there is. First of all, keep the Tiffany Theory in mind. Emphasize the positive in the relationship and try to control whatever anger or hurt brought you to this point to begin with. And never, under any circumstances, suggest that you can now be "just friends." That is insulting, and even if it comes about, it will happen in time, not in the course of a one-minute change from lovers to pals.

If you're especially worried about an emotional scene, it is possible to have "the talk" in a public place, like a restaurant. But it's kinder to allow your partner the room to express emotions honestly. Still, if you must, a restaurant is okay. Just be prepared to pay the bill.

TEN RULES FOR A CIVIL BREAKUP

1. You have to do it *in person*.
2. Emphasize the positive: "There are things I'll always love about you."
3. Don't debate small points. It doesn't matter who did what to whom.
4. Don't belittle or blame.
5. Don't pretend it doesn't hurt you too.
6. Don't downplay your partner's pain: "It's not as bad as you think."
7. Keep the children (if there are any) away, and out of the breakup.
8. Don't suggest a cooling off period. Either break up or don't.
9. It is the worst taste to break up immediately after sex.
10. Take as much time as you both need.

THE DATING QUIZ

Answer each question honestly. Five points for each correct answer.

1. It is acceptable for:
    a. a man to ask a woman on a date.
    b. a woman to ask a man on a date.
    c. any combination thereof.

Answer: C. Get over it; the fifties are over. Ask out whomever you want.

2. On a first date, who pays the bill?
    a. the man
    b. the person who did the asking
    c. the person who makes the most money
    d. the woman

Answer: B. It doesn't have to be the man. If you do the inviting, you should pay the bill.

3. A first-date proposal: "Are you busy Saturday night?"
    a. acceptable
    b. unacceptable. Tell why, and show your work.

Answer: B. Unacceptable. A proper invitation is to a specific event, like dinner, a concert, or a movie. This proposal is too vague and doesn't let the person you're asking know what they're being asked to do.

4. Your blind date is, let's say, not a super-model. You:

    a. go right ahead and continue with no outward sign that you're disappointed.

    b. smile wanly but continue with the date.

    c. contract a mystery ailment and bail out.

    d. remove the carnation from your buttonhole and go home to watch *Baywatch*.

Answer: A. You don't have to pretend she's Cindy Crawford, but you do have to be courteous. You might have a good time, and remember, you don't exactly resemble Tom Cruise yourself.

  5. You've asked a woman out on a blind date and she accepts, but proposes you meet in a public place rather than come to her home to pick her up. This is:

    a. rude.

    b. understandable.

    c. neither of the above

Answer: B. Women are justifiably cautious about letting men they don't know into their homes. Go meet at the restaurant. Be charming. Maybe she'll take you home later.

  6. It's 10 A.M. the morning of your 8 P.M. date, and you have a slight head cold. Canceling would be:

    a. understandable.

    b. unacceptable.

    c. none of the above

Answer: B. Canceling a date less than twenty-four hours before the arranged time to meet is rude and insulting unless there's an absolutely unavoidable reason. Bring along an extra package of Kleenex, but go on the date.

  7. The morning after a first date, a man should:

    a. send the woman a thank you note.

    b. call the woman on the phone.

    c. send the woman a gift.

    d. expect a note or call from the woman.

    e. any of the above

Answer: E. There should be contact the next day, and the person who did the asking in the first place does not have to be the one to initiate it. If a man takes a woman out to dinner, she is only right to thank him for it; it would be rude to do otherwise.

8. The goal of a first date is:
   a. to have sex as much as possible.
   b. to determine in one evening if this person is your mate for life.
   c. to have fun.
   d. to determine each person's interest in a second date.

Answer: D. Although C is a close runner up, the success of a first date can be measured by how much each of the people involved wants to go out together again.

9. The person you've been dating for weeks still seems uninterested in sex. Saying you'll end the relationship unless sex is forthcoming would be:
   a. rude.
   b. unacceptable.
   c. bad planning.
   d. all of the above

Answer: D. If it means that much to you and you really think this person is not going to make love to you anytime soon, don't threaten, end the relationship. But make sure you both understand each other before you take that drastic a step. Sexual blackmail is absolutely out of the question.

10. You've been divorced for six months and are ready to start dating again. The proper time to remove your wedding ring is:
    a. six months after the divorce, so go ahead.
    b. when you feel comfortable doing so.
    c. one year after the divorce.
    d. when you become engaged again.

Answer: B. If you're ready, go ahead. If not, don't. But it's a real turn-off at singles bars.

11. You're dating a single mother and her eight-year-old son asks you to take him to a movie rated PG-13. You:
    a. ask his mother first if it's okay.
    b. take him but make him promise not to tell his mother.
    c. refuse to take him.

Answer: A. The parent is in charge. Follow her lead.

12. It's that time, the relationship is, as Woody Allen put it, "a dead shark." It's not progressing, and it's time to end it. You:
    a. send your partner a very well-thought-out letter.
    b. drop an E-mail note.
    c. break up in voice mail.
    d. insist on a face-to-face meeting.

Answer: D. Accept no substitute.

Score

  0–10: Go back and read this section again. Twice.
15–30: Read it again, but only once.
35–50: Just skim. You're doing fine.
55–60: Continue on. You're ready for more.

4

Sex

THE FIRST TIME (WITH THIS PARTNER)

Black, white, green, red/Can I take my friend to bed?
—THE BEATLES, from the lyrics to "All Together Now"
by John Lennon and Paul McCartney.

Sex is a funny thing. It's also an important, sad, serious, wild, romantic, and any number of other things. It is the beginning of life and, in some cases, the center of life. It occupies a considerable amount of time and brain space, and is as elemental and basic a drive as any in the human species. It's also a lot of fun.

The problem is this: there are two uses for sex built into the species—procreation and enjoyment. But over the centuries people have built a mystique around the act itself, and ended up using it for things completely outside those two areas. People use sex for power, personal fulfillment, to hurt each other, control each other, and for commerce. And that's why people are so insecure when they make love together for the first time: they can't be sure exactly what's going on, or why.

Again, that is where the rules of etiquette—and there *can* be manners in sex—enter the picture. Keeping in mind that etiquette is a tool to help us communicate better and act more considerately toward each other, in fact, sex is probably one of the areas of life in which the vulnerable human is most in need of a Social I.Q.

Sex is, in and of itself, an awkward situation. The first time with a new partner, especially, can cause any man or woman great anxiety. We are, after all, truly naked, and any negative images we have of ourselves will surely be amplified in our minds. That mole on your thigh is going to be a blemish the size of a grapefruit by the time your mind's eye is done with it. We are exposing ourselves physically and emotionally to another person, usually one we haven't known for very long. There are good reasons for it to be daunting moment.

There is also much at stake in most cases. The first sexual encounter between new lovers can often be part of the selection process for a lifetime mate—wondering "Are we compatible sexually?" is not the least of our concerns. Suppose I say something in the heat of the moment that is uncensored, unfiltered through my usual audition process? Will my companion understand, or laugh? Will my partner be offended, or pleased? Will I feel like I've connected with someone on a basic level, or like I've been used or humiliated? Ego is a powerful thing (and *male ego* is not a proper term, since women have very healthy ones, too). New sexual partners are among the people who can help build self-esteem or completely destroy it, sometimes in a matter of seconds. One reaction in either direction can mean years of therapy.

So, as sexual ambassadors, sexual healers (to borrow from Marvin Gaye), sexual teachers, and sexual ministers, how can we do our best to put our new partner at ease, make the experience meaningful, *and* enjoy ourselves as well? Social I.Q. is on the case.

First of all, don't think only of yourself—and that goes for

both sexes. Consider how the other person feels (not like that—
I know what you're thinking!) and try to make the setting and
situation as comfortable as possible. For example:

Agree on the lights: whether they're on, and how brightly.

Don't insist that the other person undress in front of you, or
allow you to do the undressing for him or her. If he or she wants
to be alone while undressing, make the bathroom available, or
let him or her undress under the covers.

Never, *ever* point out an unflattering physical feature of your
partner's. *Ever.*

You can suggest whatever you like, but don't insist on any
one practice or another. Be sensitive to what your partner likes
to do, and doesn't.

Have condoms ready, whether you're a man or woman. It's
good manners, and just plain common sense.

After the first time, either partner is likely to have some
lingering doubts or just feelings of confusion. In these cases, it is
more, not less, important to call the next day and make sure
everything is all right. It's more likely the man should call the
woman, but each couple is different.

Again, sending a note or a gift the next day is *not* tantamount
to prostitution. You're not paying the person because you had
sex; you're thanking them for the lovely time you had, sexual or
otherwise. A note is always a nice idea. (This should not be one
of those store-bought "thank you" varieties, but something
heartfelt and handwritten.)

Keep in mind, though, that first sex doesn't mean cohabitation. A woman who sleeps at a man's house for the first time
isn't his roommate (the same applies for a man in a woman's
house), and should ask before using a toothbrush, toothpaste, or
other bathroom items. That kind of familiarity, ironically,
comes long after you've taken off your clothes and made love
with someone.

People are apt to have second thoughts after a new sexual
relationship has begun. Women especially, it seems, become

concerned that this might not be *the* man for them. That's
natural. Try to remember that he doesn't have to be *the* man for
you; it's part of the dating process, and hopefully you enjoyed
the experience. If you don't want to do it again you don't have
to, but recognize that postcoital doubts are natural, even with a
couple who turn out to be mates for life.

Sex, remember, is supposed to be an enjoyable experience. It
feels good, and as Whoopi Goldberg once said, "If it doesn't,
get another partner."

SEX FOR WOMEN

*A lady is one who never shows her underwear
unintentionally.*

—LILLIAN DAY, *Kiss and Tell*

For women, sex is a different process than it was one generation
ago. That is to say, the act itself remains the same; it has been
generally unimproved, by technology or otherwise, for quite
some time now. But the rituals and the rules surrounding it have
shifted, partly as a reaction to the feminist movement of the past
twenty-five years and partly as a natural evolution of society.

Women started gaining influence in the workplace and
equality in personal relationships relatively recently. The effects
are still being noticed, noted, explained, and even digested by
Americans. But among them is a shift in the way women decide
about sex: whether to have it, when to have it and with whom to
have it.

None of this is new: stacks and stacks of books have been
written on the subject of feminine sexuality and its general
liberation in the second half of the twentieth century. What *is*
new is the change in manners, that is, responsibilities that used

to be exclusively male are now shared, if not equally. What women have gained in sexual power—the long-overdue respect for their needs and choices—they have in some cases had to give back in the areas of courtesies and rituals.

That is not to say that the traditional has been completely obliterated. Just as many women still expect men to pay for dates, no matter what the economic balance between the couple, and some women also still see sex as a game of "they want it and we give it," rather than an exchange between two people. (Men have their own long-held beliefs, which we'll get to in the next chapter.) They think that sex is something that men have to get *from* women, rather than experience *with* women, and that leads to expectations that the man will behave one way before the first sexual encounter and another afterward. Again, this is sometimes the case, but not always. Generalizations can always be contradicted in specific cases. That's why they are generalizations.

For example, tradition has it that men should call women the day after a sexual encounter (this holds for the first several such times; after a relationship is well established, it is less important). Now, there's nothing wrong with a woman calling a man the day after, but it is a considerably rarer practice.

Women do have more responsibilities in regards to sex these days. These include:

Having condoms, or some form of birth control, available themselves. (Condoms are best to prevent sexually transmitted diseases.)

Letting the partner know what types of practices they desire. (This should be suggested gently in any situation: "You know what would be wonderful?" rather than "Hey, do *that!*")

Making it clear when they do not want to make love (men are still brought up on the idea of no means yes, so the statement must be clear).

Not faking it, because that leads to mistaken expectations on the part of the man and frustration on the part of the woman.

Not destroying self-esteem with the news that she didn't "finish." Suggest what would help rather than criticize what didn't happen.

Allowing herself to enjoy what is enjoyable and improve what doesn't work for both partners.

Women have long held a considerable amount of power in sexual relationships; they have controlled, for the most part, the frequency of sexual episodes. With the changes in sexual roles and gender roles throughout society, women have to acknowledge that both sexes can control these things. Some women express frustration with men who don't have the same intensity of sexual drive, just as another cliché claims that men complain about female partners who aren't as interested as often as they are.

It is still perfectly acceptable, and even expected, for a man to treat his partner tenderly after sex. What has changed is the acknowledgment that women should treat men exactly the same way, that it's just as important to a man to be held and kissed after sex, that the note or call the next day can come from either—or preferably—both partners.

Of course, if both partners are the type who like to roll over and fall asleep afterward, that is perfectly fine. The essential thing is not to overlook your partner's feelings, no matter which gender you are.

For men who have been hurt before, women must be healers. For those who are emotionally open but lacking in technique, women must be teachers—explain what will work for you, and be clear. Men *want* to satisfy you, they just don't know how. For all men, women are ambassadors for the feminine gender. Remember, even if this relationship doesn't last, this man will think of you as representative of women. This may not be the love of your life, but you don't want to mess him up for the next woman he meets.

There is no area in which the Tiffany Theory is more useful than in bed. Criticism here (directed at either partner) can be devastating; wrap it in Tiffany paper. Mention something your lover did that you liked before explaining why trying to twist you into a pretzel wasn't the turn-on he might have suspected it was. And keep in mind, especially if you really love this man, that you might want to sleep with him again. Make suggestions, not demands. Discuss how an already wonderful experience can be improved. And above all, do not laugh at him.

FIVE THINGS WOMEN CAN DO
TO HELP MEN IN BED

1. If you know you're going to make love, don't take off all your makeup and get into a velour robe that's going to remind him of his mother.
2. Tell him what you think is sexy about *him*. Believe me, you'll get more of it.
3. Don't be afraid to talk, but don't force it. Say what you feel.
4. Leave enough time for sex. Don't get into bed five hours before you have to get up again and tell him all you can do is a "quickie."
5. Enjoy yourself. It's the greatest turn-on of all.

SEX FOR MEN

You've got a plan of attack/That won't attract a modern woman/And you're an old-fashioned man/She understands the things you're doing.

—BILLY JOEL, from the lyrics to "Modern Woman"

Men and women approach sex differently. This probably comes as no surprise to most adults, but it does require further explanation.

The concerns of either gender entering a sexual encounter

naturally depends on the circumstances. After all, Social I.Q. was invented for people about to make love together. Every motion, every expression, every word is amplified and examined under a microscope, so everything seems much more intense, and potentially dangerous. In other words, awkward.

For women, as we've already discussed, sex is a complicated stew of emotions. Desire is no less forceful in women than men; it might manifest itself differently because of the way the sexes are usually raised. We learn a lot about sex roles (that is, gender roles) when we're children, and by the time we start thinking about sex we don't even know where the feelings come from anymore; they're just there.

Men, then, are struggling with a number of misconceptions. One is that they want sex more than women do. This isn't true, according to just about all the research done since the 1950s. Individual women may have lower sexual desire than individual men, but the reverse is just as likely to be true. Still, boys are brought up to believe that sex is something they want and something that girls don't—not "good" girls, anyway. After all, we keep hearing talk about "sexual favors," don't we? And what is a favor but something someone does for you when she doesn't really want to?

That leads to the idea that sex is something that men have to pursue and women will generally resist. That means men *expect* a refusal when they propose a sexual encounter. But this expectation is complicated by the idea, also ingrained in the male mind through popular culture (and sometimes upbringing), that some women will say no when they mean yes just to absolve themselves of the blame of wanting something they think they're not supposed to desire.

What does all this have to do with manners? Everything. Because the center of etiquette is communication; nothing makes any difference in our dealings with other people if we can't communicate—and communication is central to sex. The signals we send out to cover our basic desires and the signals we receive from the objects of those desires are a form of communication, and the better the communication, the better the encounter will be. The term *consenting adults* is one that implies communication. Consent, after all, is something that is communicated after a request has been made.

Sure, you're saying, all this is great in theory, but what does it mean in practice? Well, communication and manners are joined at the hip, and that means you need to communicate to your partner (or intended partner) exactly what's on your mind. Since sex is an area in which blunt talk can either be a turn-on or a showstopper, manners are absolutely essential. Communicate plainly, but do it with respect and empathy for what's being said and the person to whom it is being said.

For example: You've dated a woman three or four times but have not had sex with her yet. You want to find a way to ask her, but even in good-night kisses she's been somewhat reticent, holding back on passion and not volunteering anything. You're not sure whether she's not interested in physical contact or just not with you.

It's easy to clear this up, but tricky to do so without seeming like a lumbering, leering sex maniac and making your date believe that sex is all you're interested in. Your options:

1. Continue to do what you've been doing and hope you get a signal from her.
2. Nervously tell her there's "something we need to talk about" and bluntly put your cards on the table.
3. Take a somewhat more aggressive approach when you're saying good night and hope to get a positive response.
4. Start seeing other women.
5. Tell her she's the most attractive woman you've met in a very long time, but she's driving you insane with desire. Ask her whether she's been feeling the same way.

Believe it or not, the answer is 5.

The Tiffany Theory is at work again in this case. You are not telling this woman anything that's not true, but you are making it clear that you're interested in sexual activity and leaving it to her to respond. The compliment you pay at the beginning has to be worded carefully and delicately—and it had better be true.

A FEW THINGS MEN REALLY NEED TO THINK ABOUT

Foreplay. And we mean more than thirty seconds.

Condoms. As in, bring your own.

Bedclothes. Best not to tear them off her, no matter how erotic this may seem. You may want her to wear them again.

Body parts. Most women do not want to hear odes to specific pieces of themselves.

Those three words: "I love you." If you say them, you had *really* better mean them. As in, you would want to say them if she was in a velour robe that reminds you of your mother. And in another time zone, on the phone.

Cuddling. Rolling over and snoring in twenty seconds after sex is rude—unless she does it, too.

For men, the ultimate awkward situation: "It Happened Too Soon." The only thing to do is turn on the Tiffany Theory: "You were so beautiful I couldn't control myself," and then offer a return engagement as soon as possible. Depending on your age and physical stamina, this means within the hour, or half hour, or tomorrow—but as soon as possible. And yes, it happens to everybody. But that really doesn't matter when it happens to *you.*

Sex, finally, is never entirely polite, at least not by the standards set by our society. It involves physical actions that do not fit into the mold of manners. That doesn't mean for a second that people having sex can't be polite to each other in context. The key, as always, is empathy—imagine what it's like being the other person. What are her concerns, the things she cares about here? Address those, and you'll have a more pleasurable experience yourself.

After all is said and done, there is nothing quite so satisfying as making someone else happy.

HOW SEX CHANGES DATING

There's got to be a morning after.

—MAUREEN MCGOVERN, *The Morning After,* written by Al Kasha and Joel Hirschhorn

Sex takes dating to another level. It's not necessarily a higher level, but it is certainly a different level. Two people who have been seeing movies and having dinner together have now gotten much more intimate with each other, and as everyone in that situation realizes, things can never go back to the way they were before.

This is the main reason that a phone call or a note the day after first sex is so important. Both parties need some reassurance that this *wasn't* the worst mistake of their lives, that they don't necessarily have to get married now (unless they've waited until after marriage, in which case the question is moot), that they do, in the words of the age-old cliché, still "respect each other in the morning."

In today's sexual climate, too, the leap from a casual dating experience to a sexual relationship often means some form of monogamy, at least temporarily. This is only logical, as everyone knows that casual sex with a number of different partners, especially unprotected sex of any sort, can literally mean a death sentence. So couples are often taking sex more seriously these days.

It's important, of course, that all adults now understand how sex is going to change their relationship *before* they make the decision to go to bed the first time. Afterward is not the time to find out that one partner or the other has a much more casual view of the relationship. Some people become awfully possessive after an intimate encounter. Spontaneity may be romantic, but it doesn't lead to good communication, and here sooner is better than later.

For some people, sex changes everything. (I know, I've already said that about children, but keep in mind that sex can lead to children, and that's one of the ways in which it changes everything.) For others, it's simply an enjoyable activity and not an emotional experience. Either attitude is fine, as long as the two people involved share it. If they don't, there's going to be trouble. Communication, once again, is the key.

The situation is further complicated when people who have been platonic friends decide to have intimate relations. Years of confidences, trust, and mutual admiration can go out the window. Or, a long-lasting love affair may be beginning that will enrich the lives of both the partners. Only the two people involved, know if they're honest with themselves and each other, and they probably have a very good idea before they start.

Okay, you've been friends with this guy for ten years. He's helped you through some difficult times in your life; you've done the same for him. He knows you as well as anyone, and just seeing him can make you feel better. But now he wants to move the relationship into the bedroom, and you don't. Talk about your awkward situations, huh?

You can: (a) Have a heartfelt talk with him and risk losing your best friend for good or (b) give in, and risk losing your best friend for good.

Clearly, the only answer is (a). If your friend is your friend, he'll get over it eventually (or maybe soon), and understand. If he doesn't, then maybe he wasn't such a good friend to begin with. In either case, having sex with someone when you don't want to is *always* a bad idea. Don't do it.

SEX FOR MARRIED PEOPLE

Take my wife—please!

—HENNY YOUNGMAN

The cliché is that people who have been married for a while—let's say, more than a few years—are bored with each other and automatic, mechanical lovers. This certainly doesn't have to be the case.

Consider this choice: going to bed with someone who barely knows you, who is clearly going to be more concerned with himself than with you, and who hasn't the slightest idea what turns you on; or, making love with someone who has deep, intimate knowledge of your most favorite practices, areas of your body that can and can't be stimulated, where you're ticklish and where you're not; someone who not only finds you attractive enough to want sex with you but also genuinely loves you. Which one are you going to pick?

What does happen over the course of a long relationship is that life tends to interfere with love. Business, children, bills, activities, and friends distract a couple into forgetting exactly what it was that attracted them to each other in the beginning. By the end of a long day, these things also tend to make you extremely tired. Romance is not necessarily the first thing on your mind when you enter the bedroom.

What can be done to avoid an awkward situation here?

Men

- Don't neglect your partner.
- Try to seduce her every once in a while. That doesn't mean, "Hey baby, you look real hot tonight. C'mere." It does mean a few flowers, cooking her dinner, putting on music, and perhaps a gift.
- Remind her that you love her, not just want her. Give her a

kiss—a *real* kiss— when she doesn't expect it, when it *can't* lead to sex—because you love her.
- Buy her a little sexy lingerie.
- Buy something for yourself, too. Some women think boxer shorts are incredibly sexy. Don't ask me why.
- Pick a time when work isn't pressing, when she doesn't have somewhere to go—and step into her shower unannounced.
- Empathy is key—remember why you love her to begin with. That'll help.

Women

- Don't neglect your partner.
- Seduce *him* once in a while. It's perfectly wonderful for a woman to initiate sex. Men, in fact, like knowing when you want to make love.
- Give him a foot massage. See if it leads to other things.
- Put on that sexy lingerie he got you a couple of years ago that's been in the drawer all this time.
- Get something for *him* to wear. Men are hopeless at knowing what women want to see; take the decision-making process out of his hands.
- Look him straight in the eye and tell him exactly why you love him. You might remind yourself as you speak.
- Get to bed an hour earlier so you won't be so tired. You can tape *E.R.* and watch it another night. And stop drooling over George Clooney while your partner's sitting next to you.

A WORD ON SEX WITH PEOPLE MARRIED TO SOMEONE OTHER THAN YOU

Don't.

THE SEX QUIZ

Answer each question honestly. Five points for each correct answer.

1. The very idea of manners in sex is:
   a. sensible.
   b. silly.
   c. outrageous.
   d. none of the above

Answer: A. Okay, we started with an easy one. This is a book about manners; what did you expect me to say?

2. Having condoms on hand is the responsibility of:
   a. the man.
   b. the woman.
   c. both.
   d. the person whose home it is.
   e. the person who did the inviting.

Answer: C. Anyone who is going to have sex with anyone else in this day and age owes it to himself and his partner to have condoms, and use them. (Saying "himself" and "his" here does not imply that the male is the one with responsibility; it's just convenient English).

3. The man has to call the woman the day after their first lovemaking. True or false?

Answer: True.

4. The woman has to call the man the day after their first lovemaking if he doesn't call first. True or false?

Answer: True.

5. Your partner is trying a maneuver you really don't care for. You say:
   a. "Ouch!"
   b. "Hey, stop that!"
   c. "You know what would *really* be great?"
   d. all of the above

Answer: C. The Tiffany Theory is more important here than possible anywhere else. Destroy his self-esteem with A or B and you may not be able to get it back, at least for quite some time. Suggestions, however, are always welcome.

6. Women have been doing it for eons, right? Faking it is:
   a. acceptable.
   b. not great, but better than crushing his ego.
   c. unacceptable.
   d. rude.

Answer: D. (although C is also good for five points). Pretending that something is truly driving you into a sexual frenzy when it's not will encourage your partner to do it some more and frustrate him when it never works again—not to mention frustrate you, since now he thinks he *really* knows what works for you, and won't do anything else.

7. You've been dating a woman for six weeks and she seems reluctant to sleep with you. You:
   a. continue to see her without pressing the issue.
   b. have a serious talk.
   c. issue an ultimatum: sex or you walk.
   d. none of the above

Answer: D. The best thing to do is to have a talk, but don't apply pressure with how serious it is (okay, you get two points for B). Use the Tiffany Theory: Tell her she's been driving you wild with desire because she's so lovely, and ask if she's feeling the same way.

8. Here come those three words: "I love you." Say them:
   a. when you would mean it even in a nonsexual situation.
   b. when you want to get someone into bed with you.
   c. when you feel it in the heat of intimacy.
   d. all of the above

Answer: A. If you wouldn't say it on an average Tuesday at lunch, or on the phone from opposite ends of the country after a lousy workday, then you don't mean it. Don't say it if you don't mean it.

9. "It" happened too soon. You can:
   a. blame your partner: "What'd you do *that* for?"
   b. compliment your partner on how sexy she is.
   c. offer her a "rematch" as soon as you physically can.
   d. B and C.

Answer: D. (Two points each for B or C.) It's the Tiffany Theory at its best. Your partner gets the compliment (although that may be small consolation at this point), and you say you will do the best you possibly can to do better next time, and that next time will be very soon.

10. The key to good sexual manners is:
    a. empathy.
    b. sexy underwear.
    c. communication.
    d. sensitivity.

Answer: C. Not so easy, huh? Empathy and sensitivity are important, but they are parts of good communication. And communication doesn't have to mean only what you say; communication can come through expressions, gestures, and touch. Be creative.

11. You've been friends with this woman for six years, but lately you've been wanting to move the relationship into another area—the bedroom. You should:
   a. forget it, since you'll be risking your friendship.
   b. find a quiet moment and kiss her unexpectedly.
   c. consider it carefully, then talk to her about it.
   d. make your move, and use the healer role if she is not interested.

Answer: C. (By the way, if you answered D, go back and read Chapter 5 again, *carefully.*) This is a very sticky situation, because there's no going back after you've made the leap. So be *sure,* and then discuss it with your friend. If she's not interested in you sexually, you have to forget it.

12. Your partner just bought some very erotic lingerie for herself and wears it to bed one night. You:
   a. throw off your own pajamas and leap on her.
   b. get the special boxers she bought for you and put them on.
   c. tear the lingerie off her, since that's the response she's obviously looking for.
   d. smile excitedly and buy her flowers.

Answer: B. After that, you're on your own.

Score

   10–10: You haven't been out much lately, have you?
   11–20: You may be great in bed, but your manners need work.
   21–30: With a little studying, you can go a long way.
   31–40: Talk to your partner more.
   41–50: Keep on doing what you're doing.
   51–60: Are you available for dinner Saturday night?

5

Family

FAMILY: THAT AWKWARD BUNCH

Fate chooses our relatives, we choose our friends.
—JACQUES DELILLE, *Malheur et Pitie*

Few people can cause us as much joy or hurt us as much as members of our own families. Because they know us in minute detail, people in our families know our strengths and our weaknesses, our sensitive points and our emotional reserves. They have the power to protect or betray us, and while most of us can rely on our families, the sad truth is that some of us can't, and we don't always know in which group we belong.

After all, it is vulnerability, and not familiarity, which breeds contempt. If we feel exposed, that someone might hurt us at any moment, we are more likely to lash out against that person than we would be if we are at ease. When a family is really close and not just pretending to be, it is a source of support. When there are cracks in the veneer, our family can be a source of pain. And feelings and attitudes can change in an instance.

No matter which type of family you may have, there is stress involved in most family gatherings. Group dynamics are constantly shifting. Telephone calls can be tense. Holidays can become dreaded events. Or not. A lot has to do with the way we treat our family members and the way we deal with how they treat us.

That sounds an awful lot like etiquette, doesn't it? Social I.Q., after all, is the ability to take the curveballs thrown at us by other people and hit them, if not over the fence, at least into fair territory. Nobody pitches to us with more frequency than our family members, and no one knows the weak spots in our swing the way they do.

How do we find the proper way to deal with family members? It's not easy. Families are like a pond: Throw a pebble in, and there will be ripples spreading out for miles in all directions. A minor disagreement with your brother can cause bad feelings between you and your cousin for years. Turning down an invitation to your aunt's home because you have a date can mean alienating your mother. Sometimes you can't even see it coming.

The simplest way to find your route is through manners. Remember, the ultimate rule of etiquette is to treat others the way you would like to be treated yourself. If you treat your family the way you wish they'd treat you, you have a decent chance of staying in everyone's good graces most of the time. But nothing's perfect, and that's why you have to be ready all the time. You don't have to be paranoid—just ready. That's the very definition of a Social I.Q., anyway.

Here are a few awkward situations:

Your brother stops by your apartment one night and tells you he's gay. He watches your face for a reaction.

Your mother tells you she and your father are divorcing after thirty-five years of marriage. She tells you in great detail why, and it involves your father having an extramarital affair. There is a pause in the conversation as she awaits your reaction.

It's clear that your sister is not crazy about having your children in her house, although they are well behaved for two kids under seven. She's afraid something might get broken, and her expression is calling for you to do something about it.

Your cousin invites you to her house for Easter dinner and informs you that your parents and your siblings will all be there. You've always hated your cousin, and he's waiting for an answer to his invitation.

Your family and your wife's family are both inviting you for a seder the first night of Passover. Each will be insulted if you decline the invitation.

A favorite aunt dies and leaves you more money than either of your siblings. And they know it.

You visit your sister and her husband and when she's out of the room he puts an arm around your waist and tells you you're looking especially sexy today. When your sister walks back in, he removes his arm and walks to the other side of the room. Your sister doesn't seem to have noticed.

You will notice that there are no choices of possible reactions to any of the above sticky situations. There are also no answers given underneath. That's because these situations, among others, will be dealt with in the chapters immediately following this one. Consider this a reminder that they should be considered carefully, but read on. We've only scratched the surface of the trouble you can get into with your family.

And think of this: if you don't read this section, you'll always have to wonder if someone in your family already has.

TOO MUCH INFORMATION

Half the world is composed of people who have something to say and can't, and the other half who have nothing to say and keep on saying it.

—ROBERT FROST

There are few things more uncomfortable than the possession of intimate information you'd just as soon not know. Many a TV sitcom features a young adult whose parents are constantly blurting out details of their sex lives or old family secrets to make the young stars cringe. When something has achieved the level of a sitcom joke, it has become truly universal.

Quite often, our families supply us with information we'd just as soon have gone to our graves not knowing. What makes it worse is the feeling, frequently justified, that the family member telling us this intimate detail is closely scrutinizing us, trying to see what our reaction will be. No matter what we do, which facial muscle we twitch, we feel that we're being judged, and we almost always feel like we're being judged harshly.

You can't stand there like a stone and not react, but you can't think of the proper reaction, either. What to do?

Let's take it awkward situation by awkward situation:

Your parents are divorcing and your mother calls every night, clearly in pain, with bitter tales of your father's affairs and his cruel treatment of her. She wants you to commiserate, and you may sympathize, but he's still your father, and you still feel some loyalty. You don't want to agree with her negative assessment of him, even if you can see why she's so terribly hurt.

The problem is, if you *don't* agree with her; you appear to be taking your father's side in what is obviously a very personal, nasty battle. She's still your mother, too, and you don't want to appear disloyal or unsympathetic.

Clearly, you have a few choices. You can explain to your mother that you understand how painful this situation must be for her, and is for you. You can also get across the point that you are uncomfortable with the level of information she's relaying and that you do not want to abandon your father *or* her during this difficult adjustment. Make use of the Tiffany Theory, and make sure you let your mother know how much you love and respect her. But make it clear that she's pushing the envelope, and that you are not at all comfortable with what she is saying and doing.

That is the textbook answer for a situation like this: communication. It is the key to most Social I.Q. problems. But there may be some cases in which communication is not going that you have, in your life, felt this way often makes people feel worse, not better, and in difficult situations your goal is to help your friend feel better as much as you can.

Usually, what's most important when acting as a minister is to do what a minister does most often—listen. People in pain often want to "get it off their chest." They want to talk, not listen. It's your turn to listen, and do so sympathetically, remembering that in times of stress, people often say things they wouldn't say in normal conversation. Remember what needs to be remembered, and forget the emotional outbursts that may contain information you'd be happy not to have heard.

Don't be a minister who converts souls, though. People don't want you to preach to them when they're suffering; they want you to listen and help, if you can. A good minister will do precisely that.

Social I.Q. Reminder

1. Teach by example.
2. Teach only what you have learned yourself.
3. Heal with compassion, and remember the other person's motivation.
4. What you don't do can be as important as what you do—don't scold, suggest.
5. Be a minister when someone else needs one, and listen rather than preach.
6. Offer concrete solutions, or just a compassionate ear. The best teachers, healers, and ministers know that less is more.

THE TELEPHONE

Watson, come here. I need you.

—ALEXANDER GRAHAM BELL

The very first words spoken into a telephone were rude. You'll notice that Bell didn't say please when he asked—no, *ordered*—

to be possible. Suppose your mother has no one else on whom she can unload her pain. She has no siblings, and neither do you; her parents are dead and she's not able to open up this way to friends.

You still don't have to be the recipient of all this pain and painful information. Suggest to your mother—*very carefully*—that she may benefit from seeing a therapist. Make it clear that you don't believe there is anything wrong with her, but that she obviously has a lot of pain to deal with, and that trained professionals have ways to work through such situations that a lay person like yourself couldn't possibly know. Wrap that suggestion in your best Tiffany paper and hand it to her with the knowledge that you would be happy to go with her to her first session.

Now, how do you deal with your father?

This isn't exactly going to be a walk in the park, either. You now know things about your father you'd probably rather not. The image of him having an affair with someone other than your mother is not a pleasant one, and you can't get rid of it. But he is still your father. What does etiquette demand?

First, you have to search your own feelings. If you have such rage at what he's done to your mother that you can't face him, you will probably need some form of professional counseling yourself. If you think you can understand him, or at least forgive him, your father could probably use some support right now.

Without condoning what he's done, you can listen. Again, there's no reason to get into areas that are uncomfortable for you or go beyond the barriers of what you think a parent should tell a child. Simply let your father know that you still love him and will continue to do so for the rest of your life. You'll have to forge a new relationship with each of your parents separately no matter what, and it might as well be a cordial one with both of them.

In any event, nothing is gained in keeping from either parent the fact that you're in touch with the other. Secrets are at the heart of most misunderstandings, and in families, misunderstandings can be amplified to a volume that would deafen the Rolling Stones. You don't have to flaunt your support for either parent to the other, but make sure each knows that you're in contact with the other.

If you have siblings, there may be tension among you. Some may be trying to take sides with one parent or the other. Social I.Q. demands you rise above the tactic just described, take the high road, and espouse support for both parents. Don't be argumentative about it, but use your ambassador training to the fullest. Remind your brothers and sisters that both are your parents and that you intend to maintain a positive relationship with them.

What happens when your father meets you for the first time with his new—or not-so-new—love? It's bound to be uncomfortable, and you are no doubt going to have some feelings that this is the woman who broke up your parents' marriage. Remember that it takes two to tango, and marriages generally don't hit the "trouble stage" unless there are underlying problems. In any event, if you really want to keep a strong bond between you and your father, you should make every effort to include a person he has deemed extremely important in his life.

Yes, it was in horrendous taste for your father to have an extramarital affair; no manners book is ever going to condone that sort of thing (see page 94), but it's also not your business. What happens in a marriage is the province only of the two people in the marriage; even their children are only observers from the outside. Your job, as ambassador for your family, is to be as warm to this woman as you feel comfortable being, but at least warm. An effort must be made. No poisonous glances, no snarls over lunch.

The bottom line: what's done is done, and can't be undone. You have to accept the present and live in it. If this is the woman your father is involved with and you want to keep seeing your father, you're going to see her, too. It'll be a heck of a lot easier for everybody if you can try to accept that fact.

OUT OF THE CLOSET, INTO THE LINE
OF FIRE

I'm tired of being the Lesbian Formerly Known as Ellen.

—ELLEN DEGENERES

Gay people will tell you that coming out, the process during which they announce their sexual orientation to relatives and friends, is among the most difficult periods of their lives. It is an experience unlike anything heterosexuals have to deal with. In a flash, the person coming out has to discuss the most intimate part of their life and risk the rejection of the people closest to him or her.

In other words, this is the very definition of an awkward situation.

On top of that, it is awkward for both parties involved: while the gay individual is laying his entire existence on the line and hoping for a positive reaction, the person to whom he's coming out is probably straight, usually a very close friend or relative, and in all probability a little uncomfortable, no matter what his views on homosexuality might be. Even the most broad-minded person receiving such news is being presented with a side of his friend or relative that he's never had to face before, and no matter how much he's suspected, is being confronted with news that changes a great many things about someone he's probably known for years.

Because this section is about families, and because families are by definition close groups of people, let's assume that the gay person coming out is your brother. (The same condition applies if the person is your sister.) Or let's assume (depending on the sexual orientation of the reader) that you are gay, coming out to *your* brother. Examining the situation from both sides can give us an idea as to the right way of handling it.

There are few situations in which empathy is more important. If you are on the receiving end of the news, you must try to put yourself in the shoes of your gay brother. How can it feel to have to bare this particular part of your soul to someone who has known you all your life? Frightening, because the world is still woefully homophobic, and no matter how well you know someone, you can't tell how he'll react to this news. If you're straight, imagine also how embarrassing it would be to declare outloud to people you know well, exactly what you do in bed. No matter what the truth is, a mental picture will be formed. The process of coming out involves anger: Why should *I* have to go through this when *he* doesn't? And at the same time, there's pride: "I've finally managed to be myself and tell the truth!"

So, consider carefully: If you were the person giving *you* this information, how would you feel? What kind of reaction would you hope for?

Of course, you can't mask your feelings. Don't try to pretend that nothing has changed; everything has changed. Don't wince, grimace, or flinch. It's a piece of information, that's all. It's something you need to answer.

Remember, being gay isn't just about sex. It's about love; it's about who your brother *is*. Try imagining that someone told you that instead of being in love with your wife, you should fall in love with another man. Not have sex, fall in *love*. You couldn't just change, even if you wanted to. Neither can he, and neither should he. He's telling you something intensely personal and important about himself, and he's worried that you will find it repulsive.

Naturally, the response most people would want is something on the order of: "Don't worry, I've suspected all along; we're still fine." Some people, who have problems with homosexuals in general, are not going to be able to react this way. That's too bad. For them, no manners lesson or lecture on tolerance is going to be enough. It is their loss, and it is unspeakably rude, perhaps the most rude thing at all, to reject someone because you can't tolerate his lifestyle.

Now, maybe you're not that intolerant, but you really *didn't* suspect all along. Don't lie and say you did. Your mind may be reeling, but you have to react with a smile. Remember, this is the same brother you had ten minutes ago. Now you just know something about him now that you didn't before.

Tell him how you feel, that you're going to need time to adjust, but make sure that before he goes home, you embrace him and tell him that you'll never reject him because he is himself.

If you are the gay person making the announcement, you have responsibilities to yourself, but also to your brother. Remember, he doesn't know what's coming; you do. (Don't apply so much pressure that no matter how he reacts it's not going to be sufficiently positive.)

Don't stare at him after you come out, making him self-conscious about his reaction; let him react honestly. Don't scrutinize his every move with judgment in your eyes. He might not have any gay friends, and might not have a strong idea as to how he should react. Use your ambassador training to the hilt here. Remember, you may be the only gay person your brother knows well, and at least for the moment you are representing all gay people.

You, too, should be empathetic. How does your brother feel? How would you feel if, after growing up together, he told you something elemental about himself that you never knew before? A little shook up, even if it were something about which you were truly pleased. For example, if your brother told you that he had just found out that he was adopted and was from another country, you'd be a little taken aback. Wait a minute, he's not who I thought he was! Well, that's what you're about to tell *him,* something profoundly intimate about yourself that he doesn't know.

Prepare him for the announcement. Make sure your brother knows that something important is going to be discussed. There's no reason to be ashamed of what you're going to say, but it is very personal, so no one else should be present, not even if you're going to come out to someone else in your family. Don't put any more pressure on him about how he should react. Don't make it public.

In the end, both of you have to remember that you are

brothers, and that you are the same brothers you've always been. If there have been tensions, there will still be tensions. There may be an adjustment period, and it may last a while. Don't take the adjustment as rejection and don't use it as punishment. This is an important step for everybody, but it doesn't have to be a painful one.

Difficulties can continue past that initial situation, too. Let's say your parents are conservative folks, and your gay brother decides to marry his lover of the past ten years. Even though most states do not recognize the legality of the ceremony, it is an important step, just as important as when heterosexual couples commit to each other for life. But your parents don't want to attend.

They're wrong. That's all. You can tell them that; it probably won't change their behavior, but it is true. Parents should attend their children's weddings under any circumstances, and having a disagreement about lifestyle is not a sufficient excuse. It's hard enough being different in a society that demands that everyone be the same, and in a way that it has determined is right. To be ostracized by your own parents is unthinkable.

DEALING WITH RELATIVES
YOU DON'T LIKE

I despise you, and yet I'm here.

— KEVIN BACON as Tim Fenwick, to his brother,
in *Diner* written by Barry Levinson

Let's face it: you don't like all your relatives. Nobody does. Maybe your family is unusually close and you might have to look to second cousins before you find someone who truly rankles you, but they are there.

If you're lucky, you don't have to deal very often with the relatives you find annoying or downright intolerable. But not everyone is lucky. Also, even the lucky ones do have to be in a room with their less favorite relations every once in a while.

Now, I can't tell you how to make this person likable, or even how to tamp down your feelings about relatives you don't like. What I *can* show you is how a strong Social I.Q. can help you endure those occasions when you can't avoid dreaded relatives and still keep peace in your family with the people you *do* like.

TEN THINGS THAT WILL HELP

1. First, there are the things you can do whenever you have to be with anyone you find difficult to tolerate. Keep in mind that this is a single event, and it will end. Keep that end in sight.

2. Use the Ambassador Theory. In this case, it's very specific: you're an ambassador for your branch of the family, possibly even your immediate family. If the relative you don't care for is a sibling, you can be an ambassador for your own household. But you're acting as a representative, and you have a responsibility.

3. Consider why you don't like this particular person. Maybe it's something that can be improved. Maybe it's you. Dig down deep and ask yourself if you're in any way responsible. You can only fix your own portion of the problem; the rest is up to your relative.

4. As always, communication may help. If you get the opportunity to talk to this person alone, try to get past your animosity and discuss areas of common interest. Perhaps safe territory can be discovered.

5. If you really can't stand this person, keep someone you *do* like close by—a spouse, if you have one, or sibling, if there's one you're especially close to—anyone who can act as a buffer. Just make sure you're not imposing on someone who feels exactly the same way you do or you might be inviting trouble.

6. Planning is important. If you can repair things before you have to see your relative, it's possible the meeting won't

be as uncomfortable as you think. Write him a letter beforehand, but make sure it's not accusatory—make it a healing letter.

7. It can't be said often enough: use the Tiffany Theory. This time, though, use it on yourself. Think about any good points your relative has, and emphasize them in your own mind.

8. If you're really nervous about this meeting (whatever event it might be), be careful about your manner before you leave. You don't want to alienate those closest to you by being testy because you're distracted.

9. Concentrate on the pleasant aspects of the event—seeing people you *do* like, for example, and keep your contact with your disliked relative to a minimum.

10. Smile a lot, and try to make it look sincere.

Can you decline an invitation to your dreaded relative's home when the rest of your family will be there? Well, you *can,* but you will be making a very public statement, and possibly alienate closer members of the family. It might not be worth it.

The easiest thing is to accept the invitation and make the best of the event itself. For the long-term, it will keep your parents, siblings, and those relatives who are among your closest allies in the family, and perhaps in life, happy. At least it won't put them off.

Families are a strange balance of support and disapproval for many people. You are the only one who can determine what repercussions will arise from a statement like "I don't like this person and I'm not going to put up with him." Weigh the reaction you'll get before you make such a statement. If it's really worth it to you, you may have no choice. But the polite path is usually the wiser one.

If you are invited to this person's house, you must bring a gift of some sort—a bottle of wine, some flowers, whatever is appropriate—just as you would to any other person's house. You don't have to spend inordinate amounts of money, but you do have to make a gesture.

Above all, avoid the impulse to exacerbate the situation. Don't throw gasoline on the fire. You'll be happier tomorrow if you plan ahead today. And when it's over, you can go back to your life and forget the whole thing.

THE HOLIDAYS, AND OTHER LARGE FAMILY GATHERINGS

If you can't say anything nice about someone, sit right here by me.

—ALICE ROOSEVELT LONGWORTH

Even people who get along perfectly well with their families find large gatherings stressful. They're usually loud, there is a lack of control, and there is always the possibility that something will go wrong. When something goes wrong in families, it is generally discussed for all eternity, and can be a source of embarrassment and emotional agony for the person everyone has decided should be blamed.

Let's consider the elements which go into a large family gathering. Often, if you can project ahead into the event itself, you can isolate the possible trouble areas and learn to avoid them before you attend the event. Of course, it's impossible to predict *every* possible problem, but the more you can eliminate, the better off you will be.

ELEMENTS OF FAMILY GATHERINGS

Your family.   This is, of course, different for each of us, and has to be approached individually. Sorry, can't help you here.

Food.   Aside from catered affairs like weddings, family gatherings often involve members of the family bringing food. This is sometimes stressful and competitive. Keep in mind that it's just dinner, and as long as you bring something *you'd* like to

eat (and which falls into the category the host or hostess has
asked for—an appetizer, dessert, whatever), you're fine.

Alcohol.   Okay, this can be a problem. Some members of the
family might not know how to hold their liquor, and that can
lead to heated discussions, dramatic scenes, and sometimes
violence. You can't control other people, but you can control
yourself. Don't drink too much (especially if you're driving
home), and give those who do a wide berth.

A large room.   Most of the time, holiday gatherings and such
celebrations will be held in a relative's house. It's always a little
stressful to be gathering in someone else's home, since large
groups of people and most average-size homes don't mix
especially well. If you're there without children, you have less to
worry about, but you should still keep an eye out for things to
trip over or break.

Children.   There are going to be some, possibly many, and
they are unpredictable (we'll get to that subject shortly). Your
time to step in is if there is danger to a child; otherwise they are
their parents' responsibility.

If the gathering is being held in your home, obviously you
have many added responsibilities. The house must be cleaned
before the event, preferably by professionals. Any breakables to
which you're especially attached have to be put away, or at least
placed at a height above the reach of small children. Prepare as
much of the food ahead of time (and it may be a good idea to
write out a list of everything that will be served, since you don't
want to leave something in the refrigerator by mistake). Set up a
bar, including nonalcoholic drinks for those who are not
interested in alcohol.

If you have pets, and some of your guests are allergic to fur or
dander, this might be a good time to take the pet to the groomer
for the day. If you're going to allow smoking, put out ashtrays.
You might consider restricting smoking to one area of your home
to accommodate those who are uncomfortable with smoking.

When you invite the family, you have the option of doing so on
the phone, although written invitations are still best for larger
gatherings. You should specify a phone number, address, or even

an E-mail address to which to RSVP, and make sure you specify a date by which the response should come. If invitees do not respond by that date, you have every right to assume they will not be attending. It is the epitome of rude behavior not to RSVP, and you do not have to accommodate someone who doesn't.

If there is a dispute between family members, it is your responsibility to invite both parties, and not play favorites. It is their responsibility either to arrive and behave like civilized adults or to decline the invitation. Showing up and fighting is unacceptable.

When the event is a milepost in a child's life—a birthday, graduation, or similar event—and the child's parents have divorced, it is important to invite the ex-spouse. This is still the child's parent, and unless there has been such animosity that a restraining order is in place, it is not the time to play favorites. Submerge your ego for the good of the child.

Using illegal drugs at a family gathering is not only unbelievably rude, it is also dangerous, and putting the host at risk. Etiquette and the legal system agree—keep drugs out of family gatherings.

Hosting or attending a family function does not have to be awkward. A little planning and a relaxed attitude can go a long way toward enjoying the people closest to you. If a first date can be fun, so can a family gathering. Loosen up and have a good time.

CHILDREN

The hardest job kids face today is learning good manners without seeing any.

—FRED ASTAIRE

It is not reasonable to expect children to act like adults, especially polite adults. There are, in fact, so few *adults* with decent manners out there that it's downright amazing there are any children who understand what it is to be considerate and polite.

It is up to parents to teach children manners, just as they teach children everything else from birth until their children start interacting with the world. After that, it is the responsibility of the parents to steer their children toward good behavior, no matter what they're picking up at school or from friends. This goes on until the children reach legal age, at which time good manners become their own responsibility.

At this point, it may be appropriate to remember the words of the sociologist Alvin Toffler, who observed, "Parenthood remains the greatest single preserve of the amateur." In other words, *nobody* knows what they're doing, but that doesn't excuse inappropriate or inconsiderate behavior.

There are rules of etiquette which apply to children, and there are rules of etiquette which apply to parents. There are even rules of etiquette which apply to adults who don't have children, in relation to other people's children. And it's important for each group to have a firm grasp of these rules and to apply them in all situations.

Children—especially those under ten years old—are not subject to all the same rules of manners as adults. They are, however, subject to some of the rules, and some special ones that apply strictly to them.

For example, children *are* required to send thank you notes for gifts they receive, even if they say thank you to the gift-giver in person. This rule applies from the time they are able to write their names (before that, the parents should send a note in the child's name). The note does not have to be elaborate, but it is a necessity. A phone call is not an acceptable alternative.

Children are also responsible for accepting a gift graciously. Parents should instruct children to say "thank you" even if the gift is something they don't especially want, just as the children should say "no, thank you" for foods they don't like, and not "ick!"

Table manners are simpler for children, but just as important. From the time a child can successfully handle silverware he is required to use it, and not pick food up with his hands. He may not leave the table without being excused.

Bullying or hurting is simply not tolerated. Children have to be shown by their parents (or professionals, if necessary) that there are other ways to deal with anger.

Children are not allowed to interrupt a conversation between adults or other children unless a serious emergency exists.

Children should be instructed in the proper use of the telephone. When old enough, they should answer the phone with the greeting, "Hello (family name) residence." They should be sure to say "goodbye" before hanging up, and make certain there isn't anyone else in the family with whom the caller wishes to have a conversation. And for safety reasons, children should be told *never* to tell anyone who calls that they are home alone. Saying "my father can't come to the phone right now" is enough. No explanation is necessary.

With the modern age comes the idea of the "play date," something that doesn't seem to have existed when most of us were children. Instead of simply going outside to see which children are available to play, children now make plans ahead of time to play at one another's homes. Actually, the plans are made by the parents, in advance. They make sure the time, place, and duration of the play date is decided in advance, as well as the travel accommodations (who will drop the child off, who will pick the child up) and any meals that might be served during the time the children are playing together.

It is customary for the parents who send their child to another's home to host the next play date, and to schedule it as soon as possible after the first.

Children's birthday parties are subject to the same rules, generally, as adult parties. Invitations must be written and sent well enough in advance to allow for RSVP; RSVP must be done promptly, and without fail. A gift should be sent even if the invitation is declined. Otherwise, the gift may be brought to the party by the child who is invited.

It should be made clear in the invitation if parents are

expected to stay at the party, and if so, refreshments for the parents should be made available. If no such stipulation is made, it is perfectly acceptable for parents to drop their child at the party and pick her up at the time it is designated to end.

PARENTS

As a parent, you are responsible for your child's behavior. Surely, you're used to this idea, but when manners are involved, the scrutiny of society is going to be doubled. If your child does something deemed inappropriate, believe me, it will be talked about, and you will be held responsible, which is, after all, fair. You should teach your child manners.

In fact, parenting (a gerund which has cropped up in the past fifteen years, and seems to mean "being a parent") is the situation in which the teacher role is most literal, and most important. However, it's especially important to remember that you teach not only by explanation, but by example. What you do is likely to be what your child does. You are an ambassador for all grown-ups, and your child is apt to pick up signals from your actions, both good and bad.

If a child doesn't send a thank you note after receiving a gift, I don't believe the child is at fault, but I do blame his parents. Parents must insist on such a thing as absolutely basic and necessary, just like good phone manners or respect for all adults.

Gratitude, in fact, may be the most attractive of human qualities, and when being grateful for a gift given, children should express themselves in writing. It's bad enough that children spend so much of their time in front of a TV or a computer screen these days. E-mail is not acceptable, and a phone call is a very distant second. A thank you note is something that children have to learn from the start is absolutely essential.

So is polite and appropriate conversation. A child should say "excuse me" before beginning a conversation, even if there is a pause in the talk the adults are having. They should learn that "please" is the only proper way to ask for something, and that "thank you" always, absolutely follows receiving something. Parents are the strongest role models, and even if you instruct your children to use the proper words, if you don't when dealing with other people or your spouse, you're giving the child the message that this is theory, not practical application. Teach by doing.

Another way you teach by example is through discipline. No sane adult likes punishing children, but it is sometimes necessary; children need to learn the boundaries of acceptable behavior.

Still, it is desirable to teach a child what is right and wrong without humiliation. Spanking isn't as popular as it was when we were growing up (thank goodness), but is still practiced by some parents. Even in these cases, studies have shown that spanking performed by parents in private is considerably less humiliating than the discipline of a child in front of friends or other people, and making a child lower his trousers to be spanked is more destructive yet.

The point of discipline, after all, is to teach a child. If you strike a child because he hit his sister, the lesson is confused: "Why is it all right for him to hit me if it's not all right for me to hit my sister?" The point of what you're teaching is lost, and the child is taught instead that anger leads to hitting. Keep that teacher role in mind. It's the most important thing you'll ever do.

In public places, small children are apt to make a scene. This seems most likely to happen on crowded airplanes, in movie theaters, and restaurants. With infants, it's difficult to do much beyond change a diaper (preferably in the rest room, please—we do not need to see your child the same way you do), feed a bottle (or breast-feed, which is acceptable in public if it is discreet), or try to amuse a child with funny faces or attention. If that doesn't work, you have to take the child outside (except in the airplane example, of course).

With toddlers and small children, however, some rules of manners are expected, and should be followed. Parents who have planned ahead will have coloring books, small (quiet) toys, or books to amuse a child in a restaurant. Some parents on airplanes, trains, and buses like to bring a personal stereo and put the headphones on the child with her favorite music playing. In restaurants, even parents who haven't planned ahead can organize a game of tic-tac-toe on a paper placemat. The gist of the argument is that parents are responsible for keeping their child from having a tantrum or distracting other people in public. It's not our fault your child is upset, and it may not be yours, but it's your responsibility to society to deal with it and allow the rest of us the freedom to enjoy our day.

Other Adults

For the most part, adults other than a child's parents and a few close relatives (grandparents, aunts, uncles, and so forth.) do not have a strong responsibility for a child's etiquette unless they are placed in temporary care of that child. Even then, it is only in extreme circumstances that these adults should take any action.

Of course, it is always necessary to step in when a child is exposing himself or other children to danger. That's basic. But when a child who comes to visit your daughter starts to play inappropriately, hits or teases your child, where are the lines drawn between being a protective parent for your child and a buttinsky for the other child?

You have to remember that this child is not yours; it is the responsibility of his parents to instill good manners and just, appropriate behavior in him. And it is absolutely unacceptable for anyone—even a grandparent—to usurp the parent's role when that parent is present in the room. However, when you're left in charge of a child with the consent of his parent and the parent is not there, the parent is in effect giving you the freedom to use your own judgment.

Therefore, it is important that you use restraint. You want to be a protector for your child and keep her from being teased or hurt, but you don't want to embarrass her with too much parental intrusion, either. And you don't want to correct small mistakes in manners for a child who is not your own—that's not important enough for the time you're in charge of this child. Table manners, for example, are not your responsibility (although you might want to mention it—Tiffany Theory at the ready—to the parent when you drop the child off at home), but the rules of your house are to be obeyed, even by visitors, and you are within your rights to insist on this.

*However, it is never, ever acceptable for you to physically discipline another person's child.*In fact, think twice before touching another person's child for *any* reason.

Keep in mind two things—you are *not* the child's parent, and you are entitled to the same common courtesies you'd expect from any other visitor. But the bottom line is: If the parent is present, you get out of the way. Unless you see signs of physical or emotional abuse, the raising of that child is the parent's job, not yours. However, if you do see those signs, talk first to the parent, then to the authorities if you think the pattern is continuing. A child at risk needs all the help he or she can get.

Now, that awkward situation we were talking about: you go to your sister's house for a family event, and you know your sister isn't crazy about having small children playing with her breakables, making loud noises, and otherwise being children. You can tell by the look on her face that she's trying not to intervene, but she's clearly uncomfortable. And she's looking to you for help.

First, keep in mind that children are children. Your sister should plan ahead, and you should let her know that, Tiffany Theory at the ready: "You know, I was just thinking, the kids can get kind of rambunctious. Before we come over, you might want to move your favorite breakables to a higher shelf, where they can't reach them."—that sort of thing.

Second, be grateful to your sister for not stepping on your parental toes and taking things into her own hands. Children should be taught right and wrong by their parents, and she's leaving that responsibility to you. You know your kids best, and you know what works and doesn't work with them.

Beyond that, however, it is also worth keeping in mind that there are certain areas in which it is unreasonable to expect children to act like adults (in fact, it is almost always unreasonable to expect children to act like adults). Small children, under ten especially, are going to pick things up without asking, even if reminded ahead of time that they shouldn't. They're going to say things in blunt and sometimes insensitive terms. You can't stop them. The best you can do is be very careful to explain to your children before you go to someone else's home that there are different rules there, and explain to the best of your knowledge what those rules will be. If the child seems to forget the rules when you arrive, remind him. Of course, don't let him get out of hand, but don't expect him to behave like Sir Anthony Eden, either. Children are going to be children. Lighten up.

MARRIAGE AND FAMILY
(YOURS AND YOUR SPOUSE'S)

I could learn to love your mother/and your mother's sister/and if she'd visit other relatives/I swear I'd miss her/and every day before I'd go to work/I'd stop and kiss her/Maybe.

—Harry Nilsson, from the lyrics to "Maybe"

You don't just marry a man or a woman; you marry that person's family as well. That's a daunting proposition in any case, since it's difficult enough to deal with one family and its expectations. Now you have to concern yourself with two.

There is bound to be conflict. When the holidays arrive and both families expect you to show up on the same night, there's going to be trouble. When it's time to carve the turkey, and it's always been your father's job—and your spouse's father's job—

there's going to be more trouble. Duplication breeds complication.

It *is* possible to navigate these waters without any major damage being done. It takes a little finesse, a considerable amount of sensitivity and compassion, and a lot of Social I.Q. Remember your role, remember everyone else's role, and keep in mind that you're going to be seeing these people a lot, hopefully for the rest of your life. It doesn't have to be a sentence; it can be more like an advantage. But you have to know how to make it all work.

Right away, there is the first impression. The moment when your love brings you home to meet the folks, the template for so many awkward situations in life, is not considered a throat-tightening, stomach-churning one by mistake.

It's always difficult to be natural when we feel we're being judged, and that is the script for this situation: snap judgments are being made, either positive or negative, that may endure for years to come. And they are being made by people to whom your beloved has been very close starting at birth. His or her perception of you might be changing as he or she views you through the new eyes in the room. It's not easy to relax and be yourself when you feel your future is on the line.

Okay, so you're stuck in a member of the Awkward Situation Hall of Fame. Remember the rules: don't panic. You're there because someone thinks enough of you to share you with those nearest and dearest; that's an ego boost. You can overlook a little judging in order to achieve your goal for this day—to impress by being yourself. Don't pretend you're somebody else or you'll end up having to pretend for a good long time, maybe the rest of your life.

This is an ambassador situation. You're representing yourself, of course, but also your family, your gender, and your profession. Best behavior, certainly, but not abnormal behavior. As Aye Jaye writes in *The Golden Art of Schmoozing,* "Don't be on your best behavior; *become* your best behavior." It takes practice, but it can be done successfully.

Now let's say that you've married. You're a member of two

families now, and with that comes all the good and bad of one family, multiplied by two. The good takes care of itself. The awkward situations? Well, you're reading this book, aren't you?

Let's say it's your first year married, and spring has sprung. One thing you can count on for sure is that no matter which holiday you might celebrate—Easter, Passover, or anything else—both families will invite you to come celebrate. On the same day.

Especially during that first year, this is a sticky predicament. You're setting a precedent. You're picking one over the other. You're playing favorites. Each spouse, you can be sure, will vote for the family she or he grew up with.

There are three possible courses of action, each of which will get you out of trouble to some degree. You'll have to choose the one that works best for you.

You can choose one family or the other, but you have to make sure it's clear that next year, or the next holiday, the other side of the family will be favored. Also make sure that you do alternate. There may be a few hurt feelings for a while, but things will reverse when you reach the next holiday or the next year's celebration. It's important not to play favorites, but at some point you may appear to be doing so. The only way to get by is to make sure you favor the other side of the family when the next opportunity arrives.

You can accept the first invitation you receive, but ask if the other side of the family is welcome, too. This isn't the most successful road, but it will show your fairness is intact.

Or you can jump the gun and hold the celebration yourself, inviting everyone in both families. Yes, it's a lot of work, but you can't get anyone mad at you by asking them to dinner.

The New Family

Today's family unit is not like those of thirty years ago, or even twenty. Society's changes have changed the family, and vice versa. Today, the idea that one set of parents raises its children and stays together forever is almost quaint.

Let's say a man with children from his first marriage decides to remarry, and the woman he's marrying has children from *her* first marriage. The Brady Bunch? Not necessarily.

You may be shocked, but every postdivorce family is not as happy and conflict-free as the Bradys (who were, it should be noted, the family of a widow and a widower). Imagine if Mr. Brady decided to favor Marcia and Jan over Greg and his brothers.

Of course, it's not nearly that neat most of the time. Usually, children of a divorce are in the custody of one parent—often their mother—most of the time. It's more likely that in this case the man would be living with his new wife's children and not his own.

Does that mean that the children from his first marriage should see their paternal grandparents less often than the new stepchildren? That there should be more pictures of the wife's children in the home? That the children who live in the house, and not with the ex-wife, should be given better Christmas gifts?

It's a sad fact that some stepfamilies favor one set of children or the other, and it's a disgusting, horrible fact as well. There is no excuse for it. Children must be treated equally or their parents are doing them a huge disservice.

There is no easy way to blend two families, but making one the "good" family means the other is "bad," and that, to put it mildly, is unacceptable.

MISUNDERSTANDINGS

Paul Revere? An anti-Semite bastard . . . he kept yelling,
"The Yiddish are coming! The Yiddish are coming!"
—MEL BROOKS, as the Two-Thousand-Year-Old Man

Sometimes you get into trouble with your family, and you didn't even do anything wrong. It's the appearance of a slight, or something that seems to be insulting, that creates tension. You might not even know it, but suddenly a family member is acting prickly when you're around.

Naturally, communication is key, but you can't communicate all by yourself, and some members of your family might deny that they are upset, despite all appearances to the contrary. You can usually trace the source of the behavior to a recent family event. For example:

Your favorite aunt, ninety-nine years old, passed away recently, and you are mentioned in her will. So are your brother and your cousin. But when you reveal the amount you are receiving, it's clear that your brother and your cousin are getting less than you did. Instant tension.

Okay, first of all, you shouldn't have mentioned how much you're getting. Sure, you assumed they would be receiving the same amount, but you can't be sure, and it's in poor taste to discuss such things, anyway. By keeping your mouth shut you could have avoided the whole situation.

But if one of your relatives is gauche enough to ask the amount, do you have a choice? Yes, you do. You can say that it's bad taste to ask such a question. The problem with that answer is, no matter what the situation, everyone will assume that you're getting more than they are. Otherwise, why wouldn't you tell?

Clearly, this situation isn't your fault. You didn't ask your aunt to leave you more money than your relatives. You might not even know she did until after the reading of the will. Still, the reality of the situation is that your aunt is dead and you will be the object of everyone's anger.

What can you do? There are a few tactics. One is the time-honored "let time take care of it" theory, which means you simply ignore the situation and hope that in time everyone will calm down. Sometimes, this is one of those rare occasions in which ignoring a problem can actually help it go away. Sometimes, however, it's not.

When you can't bear the thought that people are angry with you, you might be unable to let enough time go by for the family to cool down. If so, you have to weigh your move carefully. This is the Tiffany Theory at its most critical. You have to be very careful not to accuse, but to explain—not to complain but to heal. Use your role as a healer. Remember, you aren't trying to make yourself feel better, you are trying to make your *family members* feel better, so they will be able to forgive you for something that isn't your fault. Is it fair? Not necessarily, but it does work, and it will, ultimately, remove some of your own discomfort.

Let's examine an even more awkward situation, and again one that is not of your own doing. This situation will not go away by itself, ever.

You are at your sister's house for a visit, and she leaves the room for a moment. Her husband, with a strange look in his eye, puts an arm around your waist and tells you that you're looking "especially sexy" today. Before you have a chance to respond, your sister walks back in, the arm disappears from your waist, and there isn't so much as a flicker of awareness on your sister's face, nor another signal of anything from your brother-in-law.

The obvious impulse would be to ignore the incident, "let it slide," and assume that you misinterpreted his intentions. But there's trouble in your sister's marriage, and it's been brought to your door. To ignore it is to betray her.

Still, do you make a scene at the moment she walks back into the room? No. Compose your thoughts. Don't even say anything while you're visiting (although you may want to develop a headache and cut the visit short). Wait until you are alone with your sister and then tell her in exact terms—only facts, no interpretation—what happened. Let her decide what to do.

If she chooses to believe that it was an innocent remark—and if nothing ever happens again—you have done your duty and she has made her choice. If your sister decides that this is a major problem, her husband might deny anything like that happened, or might blame you for any action your sister takes. You have to be prepared to deal with those possibilities. But you know what happened, and you have an obligation to report it—that's all. Don't start with, "Your husband made a pass at me." That's interpretation. Do start with, "There's something that happened when you were out of the room," and then explain exactly what he did and what he said—not what you were thinking, and not your guess as to what it meant. Just what happened. Be like Jack Webb on *Dragnet*. "Just the facts, Ma'am."

If the incident is repeated, you have to report it again, and let your brother-in-law know in no uncertain terms that such familiarity is not welcome and will not be tolerated. If he continues after that, you may have to be sure not to be alone in a room with him.

Nobody ever said families were easy.

THE FAMILY QUIZ

Answer each question with the help of the previous chapters. Five points if you don't have to go back and check; three points if you do. Add up your score at the end.

1. Your parents are divorcing. Your mother tells you your father was having numerous affairs. You tell her:
   a. that she's right, and that he's a horrible man.
   b. that you don't know both sides of the story, and can't comment.
   c. that this information is not something a parent tells a child.
   d. that you love her.
   e. all of the above

Answer: Five points for B, C, or D. No points for A or E. Tell her you're not comfortable with this information but you love her, and you don't want to judge either her or your father.

2. Same divorce, other parent. Your father calls and asks you to come have lunch with him and his new girlfriend. You:
   a. hang up on him for cheating on your mother.
   b. ask if you can have lunch with him and *not* his girlfriend.
   c. accept and grit your teeth.
   d. none of the above

Answer: D. If you want to have a relationship with your father, you can't do any of these things. He's starting a new life, and you'll choose either to be a part of it or not. The closest answer to a correct one is C, but you can't grit your teeth, you have to try to be hospitable to your father and the woman in his life.

3. When a gay person decides to come out to a family member, the ambassador role is one that falls on:
   a. the straight individual.
   b. the gay individual.
   c. both
   d. neither

Answer: C. Everyone is worried about being judged, but in this situation, both parties are being scrutinized carefully, and by each other. The gay sibling, for example, is now a representative for all gay people, and the straight sibling is doing the same for heterosexuals. Best behavior is advised on both sides.

4. You're gay and about to let your family know. You should:
   a. gather them all together and make an announcement.
   b. tell each one privately.
   c. send a letter.
   d. none of the above

Answer: B. While such things are personal and left to the sensibility of the person making the announcement, it is kinder to each family member to do this sort of thing personally (although parents, for example, might want to hear the news together). There's enough scrutiny going on between two people; having to worry about group dynamics complicates the matter unnecessarily.

5. On those occasions when you have to spend time with relatives you truly can't stand, you should use the Tiffany Theory:
   a. on yourself.
   b. to decline the invitation.
   c. on your relative.
   d. all of the above

Answer: A. Use the Tiffany Theory in your own mind to

make the visit tolerable. Try and think of the things (however insignificant) you like about this relative, and in your own mind emphasize them while the things you find hard to take are in evidence around you.

6. You're invited to a despised relative's home and you can't decline the invitation without causing a major family incident, so you're going. You:
   a. show up late, leave early and eat as little as possible.
   b. bring a gift, but make sure it's obvious it's a cheap one.
   c. wrap up something you have around the house.
   d. bring a gift and make it as expensive as possible to emphasize how classy you are.
   e. none of the above

Answer: E. Yes, you do have to bear gifts, even when visiting people you don't like. It's common courtesy. No, you don't have to make it incredibly expensive, and you can't bring something from home or an obviously cheap token. Make it something very simple and priced within your budget. In this case, it's less the thought than the gesture that counts.

7. When you're hosting a family gathering yourself and two family members are feuding, you are responsible for:
   a. monitoring their behavior.
   b. keeping them in separate rooms, if possible.
   c. inviting them both.
   d. gathering a family consensus on which one to exclude.

Answer: C. You invite both parties. It's not up to you to choose between them, and it's not your responsibility to make them behave. They're adults, and you should expect them to behave like adults. (Well, you can hope they'll act like adults, anyway.)

8. By the same token, when hosting a birthday party for a child whose parents are divorced:

a. do not invite the ex-spouse for fear of ruining the child's day.
b. invite the ex-spouse, unless a restraining order is in place.
c. have the ex-spouse over separately.
d. have the ex-spouse celebrate the birthday during a planned visit.

Answer: B. For the sake of your child, swallow your anger for a day. Both parents—biological parents—should be there unless there's serious reason to fear for anyone's safety.

9. While we're discussing children, children are:
    a. absolutely required to send thank you notes.
    b. not subject to all the rules of etiquette.
    c. expected to RSVP for parties.
    d. all of the above

Answer: D. Children don't have to follow *all* the rules, but they do have to follow some of them. Thank you notes and RSVP are not negotiable.

10. You're taking small children out to dinner. In order to be courteous to the other patrons of the restaurant, you:
    a. prepare with coloring books and other diversions.
    b. choose a child-friendly restaurant.
    c. make the children sit with their hands folded until the dinner arrives.
    d. remove the children if they cause a scene.

Answer: Anything but C. Kids are kids, and you, as the adult, have to help them through what can be a difficult situation. You also have a responsibility to other adults, and that means not letting the kids create an uncomfortable scene.

11. Someone else's child is at your house playing with your child, and he's acting like a bully, hitting your son and bossing him around. You:

a. call the child's parent and ask to have him taken home.
b. tell your child to hit back and defend himself.
c. talk to the child, but don't touch him at all.
d. step in for your son.

Answer: A combination of any but B. None of these things is exactly the right answer, but give yourself five points for A or C. Two points for D, since that's a little vague. You don't want to embarrass your son, but you do have to defend him. Tell the child's parent when he or she picks him up.

12. You're newly married and your spouse's family has invited you for Christmas Eve, which is traditionally a night you spend with your family. Uh-oh. You:
   a. accept the invitation, asking if your family can attend too.
   b. offer to host the event yourself.
   c. decline the invitation, saying this is a family tradition.
   d. none of the above

Answer: A. It's too late to host the event yourself; you've already been invited. Saying that your family traditions are more important than those of your spouse is inconsiderate and bound to cause trouble. You might think of hosting the event for both families next year, but in this case, you have to accept the first invitation you receive, while gently suggesting that both families be involved. Failing that, see your family on Christmas Day.

13. Your mother invites you to dinner once a week, and hasn't invited your brother for three months. Your brother is starting to resent you. You:
   a. step in and ask your mother to invite your brother along.
   b. decide this isn't your problem and do nothing.

    c.   talk to your brother, letting him know it's not your fault.

    d.   none of the above

Answer: C. It's not up to you to get your mother to make invitations if she has some problem with your brother. It is up to you to mend the relationship between you and your brother. Communication is the path to understanding. Communicate.

14. Your brother-in-law makes a veiled pass at you and your sister doesn't appear to notice. You:

    a.   slap his face and leave the house.

    b.   inform your sister that her husband tried to sleep with you.

    c.   stay out of a room alone with your brother-in-law.

    d.   talk to each one privately, making sure your sister knows exactly what happened, and that her husband knows it must never happen again.

Answer: D. You're not causing trouble; you're preventing it. Your brother-in-laws's behavior continues, you might consider C.

Score

    0–15: Are you sure you *have* a family? Did you say the *Manson* family?

  16–30: Family counseling is always an option.

  32–50: See the turkey scene in Barry Levinson's *"Avalon,"* you'll understand.

  52–60: Congratulations! You're qualified to go to your next family reunion.

  62–70: Congratulations! You're qualified to come to *my* next family reunion.

6

Friends

SITUATIONS

*We cherish our friends not for their ability to amuse us,
but for ours to amuse them.*

—Evelyn Waugh

There are few things more important in this life than our
friends. These people, whom we choose to keep close to us
through the years, can be more prominent in our lives than our
family. Some of them know our most intimate secrets, our
fears, and our weaknesses. They have been there when we
needed them and we have done the same for them. They are
essential to our lives.

Still, any human interaction is fraught with the possibility of
awkward situations. What happens when a friend marries
someone you can't stand? What if a friend suddenly isn't as
friendly as she used to be? We've already discussed the possibility of friends becoming lovers, but what happens when two
of *your* friends become lovers, and you start feeling just a little
left out? If an acquaintance starts entering "friend territory" and

you're not sure you're happy about it, how do you react? What happens when your old friends don't accept your new friends?

I find human behavior fascinating because of its infinite complications. Every time two people strike up a conversation, absolutely anything can happen. Think of the first time you met your spouse. Your best friend. Your employer. Were there signs that this seemingly casual conversation might change the course of your life? Maybe, but I'll bet not. In most cases, our lives change at points that we can't predict, so we always have to be at least a little alert, aware that we might be looking into the future, even when it seems like a passing moment.

The beginning of a friendship, especially, is hard to gauge. After all, many of us meet lovers and spouses through dating, sometimes even by being fixed up, so we're on our best behavior to begin with. We're aware that the person we meet tonight might play a major role in our future. We meet our employers at job interviews, when it is quite clear exactly what the stakes are and what kind of behavior is required.

But nobody fixes up friends. We strike up conversations at random, in school, at business functions, in line at the movies— anywhere. Where did you meet your best friend? In high school chemistry class, where you might have been placed in neighboring seats strictly by chance, or by height? A random selection may have introduced you to someone who will be your confidante for decades to come ·

It's a given that a good friend is to be cherished as much as a lover, treated like family, and thought of before yourself. Friendship is the most precious gift on this planet, and is often overlooked. Our friends are our friends, and we don't often consider what that means. But when we let that comfortable feeling bleed over into neglect, or we feel neglected ourselves, friendship can be in jeopardy. Because it is so important, real friendship is something that is worth fighting for.

It doesn't have to get to that point, however. Social I.Q. exists not only to get us through awkward situations, but to prevent the ones that can be really damaging to ourselves and those we care about the most. With careful practice and a little attention, we don't ever have to arrive at a situation that could mean the end of a friendship. After all, prevention is the best medicine.

Read on, and keep in mind that what applies to your friends applies to you, too. Expect what you give to come back to you, but don't demand anything you're not willing to give yourself. After all, friendship is a two-way street.

OLD FRIENDS

You and me, Buddy, we got secrets she'll never know. Those new friends will never be as good, because we've got a history.

—STEVE GUTTENBERG as Eddie, in "Diner,"
written by Barry Levinson

Sometimes, you don't even remember how you met. Still, you can't imagine life without them. It's no accident that the phrases "oldest friend" and "best friend" are often interchangeable. The people we know we can trust, those who have proven themselves to us time and again, are the ones whom we most often rely on for emotional support. That's a great asset, and sometimes an enormous responsibility.

Yes, friendship is a blessing of tremendous import in our lives. It can also be a labyrinthine relationship that can include virtually every emotion, from elation and lust to love, betrayal, and grief. Everything that can happen in a romantic relationship is possible in a friendship, although sex, if it enters the picture, often makes the relationship cross from friendship into romance and moves it to another level.

See what I mean? Complicated.

Friends tend to come in groups. Common interests, geography, even a time period (college friends, high school friends, work friends) can all be contributors to this aspect of a friendship. It becomes tricky when groups of friends intersect, that is, when a person encourages other members of one group to interact with members of a second group.

Friendships can also wear, fray and stretch to the breaking point. The idea that people grow apart is as active in platonic friendships as in romantic relationships. How many of the people who were vital to your existence in high school are part of your everyday life today? If you're over thirty, and the answer is more than one, you are either very lucky or hopelessly mired in the past.

Still, that one friend is probably among your most cherished. He knows you as well as anyone can, has been through the best and worst times of your life, and stayed with you. That's a huge commitment, and one that is made willingly, with no promises of anything in return. You can trust this friend with any secret, any fear, and not worry that trust will be betrayed. This is truly a time-tested relationship.

So, what are the limits? Is there anything you should never tell anyone, aside from a spouse? Is placing your soul in someone else's care a reasonable thing to do? Is it fair to the other person? Is it safe for you?

Obviously, many of the answers to these questions can be summed up in the phrase, "it depends." It depends on you, your friend, and the trust you're placing in his or her hands. It's one thing to discuss your new relationship with an old friend; it's quite another to reveal a childhood trauma, like parental abuse or incest, and that decision has to be made knowing all the circumstances. Only you know what you feel comfortable revealing and what you don't. In some very serious cases, it may be best kept between you and your therapist. Never be afraid to seek help when you need it.

Secrets and Friends

Your friends are bound to know some of your secrets. Your old friends are bound to know your older secrets. They were there when a lot of your secrets were revealed, and when some of your most embarrassing moments occurred. You can't hide these things from the people who have known you the longest.

But your current secrets—which include anything you haven't revealed, no matter how old the information might be—are a different matter. They are things you have to make decisions about, and each one requires a separate decision. You are having an extramarital affair. Do you tell your best friend? Is this information you feel safe imparting to another human, no matter how long-standing the relationship might be? Is it fair to burden your friend with this kind of devastating—or potentially devastating—secret?

It's not fair, under *any* circumstances, to inflict unwanted responsibility on anyone else. It's bad etiquette, bad manners, and bad friendship. So if you think that your friend would sincerely be happier not knowing your secret, don't tell him or her. Your needs are important, but so are your friend's.

By the same token, it's going to bother some friends when you *don't* share your most intimate concerns with them. Keeping things from the people who care about you most is hard, but sometimes it's necessary. Share information with your friends when you think they need to know it, when they can handle it, when you need to unburden yourself, or when you think your friend would sincerely be hurt to know you *didn't* share it.

Secrets are never easy things. They're one of the reasons we need our friends so badly.

When Friends Marry

Marriage can wreak havoc with friendships. It doesn't have to; there are many cases in which marriage actually strengthens ties between friends. But it can't be denied that committing to one person for the rest of your life can cut down on the amount of time you have to go bowling.

There are three situations in which marriage can enter a friendship, and any one of them has the potential to improve or destroy the bonds between people. The difference between "improve" and "destroy" lies in the way the friends prepare ahead of time for the change that's most assuredly coming in their lives. Preparation, of course, is one of the most basic pillars of Social I.Q.

One friend is getting married. The introduction of a new person—the spouse—into the friendship is the difference here. If you're the friend headed to the altar, you have to take careful steps ahead of time to ensure that you can maintain a friendship while you enter a marriage.

First, let's assume you have introduced your soon-to-be-spouse and your long-standing friend. Great. If they get along, you will have few problems in this area. If they don't, you'll have to make it clear to each that you intend to keep both relationships alive and healthy, but it also has to be clear to both the spouse and the friend that a marriage is a lifetime commitment, and it will take precedence over the friendship. The marriage, in other words, is going to be the number one commitment from here on. That doesn't mean the friendship is doomed, but it does mean the marriage will have top priority. You'll do your best to accommodate your friend, but your spouse is going to be the center of your life.

Two of your friends are marrying. The group dynamic is about to undergo a serious shift, or did when the two became a couple. You may still be working on some issues. You may be feeling left out, no longer part of the group, since they are forming a smaller, very close group of their own. Are you losing two friends as each of them gains a spouse? Not really. Yes, there are changes when two members of any group decide to marry. They are by definition excluding all the other group members by declaring their intention to be more important to each other than to anyone else. They are taking a larger group of friends, and creating a smaller group that will be a family. But that doesn't mean you're being abandoned, merely that your role is changing, and that is a natural function of life. Our roles are constantly changing in all areas of our lives as we get older and take on, or cast off, responsibilities.

What's your job now? Mostly, to continue to be a friend. As the marriage progresses, or even as it begins, there are the inevitable stresses between the husband and wife. You have to be careful not to be seen taking sides. If it's going to be uncomfortable, ask each one of your married friends not to discuss anything about the marriage with you. Remember, every story has three sides: his, hers, and the truth. You'll never know the truth.

If you're feeling left out, like you're no longer as vital to their lives as you once were, try to remember: You are just as vital to them, but they have become more vital to each other. You are not being left out so much as each of them is being let into the other's life more completely. It's not a friendship issue, and you shouldn't feel abandoned. If you do, and you think you have specific examples of inconsiderate behavior on your friends' part, talk to them about it, either together or separately. Explain your feelings, and try to get them to see things through your eyes.

You're marrying a friend. Try and keep your other friends in focus. Read the second situation, above, and put yourself in your friends' place. Talk to your almost-spouse about it, and make plans to invite everyone over soon. Make it clear that this is not the end of the friendship, but the beginning of your marriage. The two things don't have to be at odds with each other.

Best Friends

Some people have many friends, but no best friend. Some people have only a best friend. It's only a matter of opinion, but I think the second group is better off than the first.

A best friend is a very special person. This is someone with whom all pretense can be dropped, someone who has been there for enough of the highs and lows of your life that there's nothing that could surprise him anymore. He's seen you, warts and all, and still wants to hang around with you. That's a special quality, and something to be cherished and nurtured as diligently as you possibly can.

Does having a best friend mean your other friends are inferior? Of course not. Nobody needs to be left out because you have a special understanding, a communication, with another that is easier and more comfortable for you. In a way, it's the opposite of a marriage—it's a lifelong commitment but *doesn't* assume total immersion from either party. The lifelong commitment is often unspoken, and assumed only because both friends understand that it exists without their creating it. Best friends aren't as much work as a spouse, but there is rarely any sex involved, either.

"Best friend" is also not an official title. Some people have a few "best friends," however that may seem to fly in the face of the word *best*. Some people have a best friend and never use the term.

What can be a problem, though, is that a best friend, by definition, is the person on whom you can rely to understand your foibles better than just about anyone else. That may mean you will take your best friend for granted, because you know that if you treat other people the way you treat her, she will become upset with you. Quite often you will respond better to people about whom you care considerably less.

Don't overlook your best friend because she's your best friend. Yes, she'll understand when you don't have time to be polite, but be polite anyway. Put in extra effort to spend time with her even when you're up to your eyebrows with work and don't have time to tie your shoes. Remember what the words *best* and *friend* mean. Take the time to consider those two words, and you'll find yourself treating her better. In other words, use your Social I.Q. and you'll find yourself treating other people more considerably by reflex. And everyone will be happier for it.

NEW FRIENDS

The eternal quest of the individual human being is to shatter his loneliness.

—Norman Cousins

Meeting someone and striking sparks is one of the most exciting experiences in life. If we do indeed search for others with whom we can share our lives, we will clearly have a sense of accomplishment, relief, and joy when we do connect with another person.

This connection does not have to be romantic. In fact, most of the time it's not. With people of the gender to which we're not sexually attracted, friendship is the natural outgrowth of mutual interests, a shared sense of humor, a similar view of life. With members of the other sex, such shared experiences and temperaments can be romantic, but more often will be the basis for a possible friendship.

Most people don't have an enormous number of romantic partners in their lives (that is not to say sexual partners, but people with whom we truly fall in love), but they can have unlimited numbers of friends. And that beginning period, when the common ground between two people and the warm feeling of mutual interest is first noticed, can be the most exciting and wonderful rush of all.

New friends are a combination of possibilities and pitfalls. You can tell immediately that you are comfortable with this person, and you can find yourself falling into interesting conversations about mutual interests within minutes of meeting. But it's just as possible that there are "deal breakers," subjects upon which you will never agree, and that may mean you can't go beyond merely smiling and nodding when you pass each other in the street. For some people, a difference in political views will be a problem; for others, the same amount of difference will matter much less. Others have trouble with differences in religion, humor, taste, and profession. Some people have no deal breakers, and will simply accept everyone for whatever he or she might be. But these people are alas, rare. And you won't know until you pursue the matter further.

On first meeting, it's not polite (and it's just a bad tactic) to grill someone on his political, sexual, and professional views. This rule applies to romantic situations as well as friendships. The person undergoing the scrutiny will naturally feel pressured and insulted. It's better to allow things to continue naturally and let the touchy topics arise as they may. Maybe they never will.

If you are the person with make-or-break characteristics for a friend, you still can't send trial balloons out conversationally the first time you meet a new person. It's rude, and it won't work very well. What you have to do is mention, along the line, that you are interested in politics, religion, or whatever area is your defining characteristic, and see how the person replies. Don't turn the situation into an interrogation or you may miss out on having a friend for life.

A Clash of Friends

Sometimes having new friends complicates matters with old friends. Your long-standing friends might feel like they're being replaced, or that you're trying to force someone into their lives when they're not necessarily all that receptive to the idea. Sometimes your new friend might not want to be immediately included in a group that has a much longer history. People are pesky that way; they don't like your making their life decisions for them.

You, on the other hand, are entitled to choose your friends. Just because you have a long-standing group of close buddies doesn't mean you can't add people to your life. It's the mixing of the two that can cause trouble.

In many ways, friendship is like romance: You can't force people to like each other, no matter how clear it is to you that they have a tremendous amount in common. (In fact, sometimes it's that very common ground that will create animosity; you can't predict these things.) All you can do is conduct introductions and watch to see what happens.

If your friends hit it off on both sides, great. You've created a larger congenial group. If they don't, well, you tried. But that's it. They don't get along, and you have to accept that.

Still, you can continue to be friends with both sides. There's no reason not to.

Awkward Situation: You've become friendly with another couple, the parents of your daughter's best friend. But now the two girls are having a serious argument and refuse to speak to each other. What happens to your friendship?

Social I.Q. Solution: Children and teenagers are, rather inevitably, children and teenagers. You have to prepare yourself for the sure-to-come arguments *before* they happen. Discuss this with your friends, and assure each other that there will be no conflict between you because your children are having a disagreement, even if they never want to see each other again.

Complication: You think your daughter is right, and they think their daughter is right.

Social I.Q. Solution: Hopefully, you've faced this possibility when discussing a hypothetical argument between the girls. If you haven't dealt with it ahead of time, though, this is certainly the time to get to this discussion. But...

Don't discuss specifics of the fight. "Your-daughter-did-this-to-my-daughter" arguments are sure to erupt, and that's exactly what you're trying to avoid.

Do lay the groundwork for your own behavior, meaning that of all four parents involved. Make sure that among the four of you, no sides are taken, and no attempts are made to intervene in the argument. If you have social plans with the other parents, or want to make them, go ahead. If the children are dead set against doing anything together, don't include them in the plans; make it a "parents' night out."

Don't let the argument of two kids spoil an adult friendship. It's important to support your child, but it's not necessary to fight her battles for her. Taking sides at the expense of your own friendship because you think not doing so is a betrayal would be foolish. Children's arguments are, by nature, childish. Don't get involved.

Stages of a Friendship

Friendships have lives of their own. They have beginnings, middles, and sometimes endings. The beginning can be subtle, almost unnoticed. Sometimes you don't even realize someone is your friend until he's been hanging around for months. Then, suddenly, you wonder how you lived your life without him all those years.

By the way, if it sounds like I'm talking about friendship in the same terms as a romantic relationship, that's because I am. We fall in love with friends the same way we do with people we might marry. The process is very similar, and the issues are often the same. Where in some cases, romance is complicated by sex and cohabitation, in some cases, friendships can be similarly colored by the romantic entanglements of the people involved. That doesn't mean two friends falling in love, but it does mean two friends who have active romantic lives. The cast constantly changes, but the play remains the same.

The second stage of a friendship is, if you're lucky, the longest. It occurs when you and your friend are going through life, together. Often, it can involve major milestones: love, marriage, parenthood, grief, and illness. At this point, you and your friend will sometimes be firing on all cylinders, operating like a well-oiled machine. You won't have to talk to communicate. You'll be able to anticipate each other's moods and reactions. The road will be straight and smooth.

Then you'll hit a bump in the road. Out of nowhere. Unexpected and hard. You don't necessarily ever find out where it came from, but suddenly there's tension between the two of you. It might be external, that is, from something unrelated to your friendship, like another person (a spouse, for example) or a life event (an illness or a professional problem). But your friend isn't acting like he used to—or you're not. There isn't as much laughing. There's not that much communication. The phone stops ringing.

These are the times you have to work hardest. Now, it's possible that the situation could have been avoided by working hard before. If, for example, your friend starts to feel you are not paying enough attention to her, or that you only call when you need a ride to the airport, a frank conversation long ago, or a little more attention on your part, would have gone a long way.

But let's assume that it's gotten this far: your friend isn't calling anymore, and the past few months haven't exactly made you feel like rushing to her side, either. You need to take a long, hard look at this friendship now. If you decide it's worth saving (and most are), you have to take steps. Now.

First, do your evaluating. To diagnose the illness, check the symptoms: When did you start feeling the friendship was ailing? What tipped you off? Your friend stopped calling? He's making sarcastic comments that don't seem like the old-fashioned joking around you are used to? Little things started annoying you about him, or he complained about little things you do? Sounds like at least one of you has a problem with the amount of attention being paid—not enough, on one side or the other.

Second, make a decision. Is this friendship worth rescuing? There's a very serious litmus test: if you don't care whether the friendship is worth saving, it's probably not. All others are.

Now, be empathetic; be an ambassador; be a minister; be a healer. Put yourself in your friend's hat. How do you think she feels right now? Why? What would make him feel different than the way he used to about you?

Pick up the phone. Somebody has to be the one to do it, and you're the healer. Call, but make absolutely sure not to be combative or argumentative. Just say you think a good talk is in order.

Talk; use the Tiffany Theory, the Ambassador Theory, the minister and healer roles. Explain how you've been feeling, but listen to your friend's side, too. Apologize if you've been neglecting your friend. Promise to try to do better. Begin by picking up the check for dinner.

Really try. Lip service isn't going to buy you more than a week or two; an honest effort will help you keep a friend for life.

Demand your due, too. Don't settle if you think you've really been wronged here. The goal, remember, is not to punish or to force an apology, but to save the friendship. Do your best to make your friend understand how you've been feeling, and why. And then explain—without sounding like you're issuing an ultimatum, using the Tiffany Theory at its best—what you think needs to be done to heal the friendship. If it takes effort on his part, explain what effort you need. If it takes effort on your part, make the effort.

Friendships are like everything else in life. If they come too easily, they're not as lasting, and not as good.

ACQUAINTANCE TO FRIEND: A LINE IS CROSSED

All changes, even the most longed for, have their melancholy; for what we leave behind us is a part of ourselves; we must die to one life before we can enter another.

—ANATOLE FRANCE

Every change in human relationships requires consent. Friends who become lovers must both agree to become lovers; lovers who become married clearly agree to that step. You can change yourself with no one's approval but your own, but you can't change your status in someone else's life unless they will let you do so. The only thing you can do effectively on your own is leave.

And so we come to a chapter that is all about one awkward situation, in which one person wants to become something other than what he is in another's life—an acquaintance, someone familiar but nothing more—and take on the role of friend. It's very similar to the leap that friends take when they become romantically involved, but with one enormous difference: the friends are already familiar and comfortable with each other; they have made the adjustment to being friends. This step is much less surefooted, because you don't know the person with whom you're dealing well enough to predict a reaction.

First of all, it should be noted, that most of the time this type of transition occurs naturally. People who just sort of know each other become friends all the time, with no prodding and no special steps taken. They wake up one morning secure in the knowledge that they have a friend. That's the easiest thing on the planet to do, short of breathing.

In a minority of cases, though, a conscious effort is made to change the relationship. One person decides he's interested enough to try to establish a friendship with someone he knows casually. It doesn't mean that he has to announce his intentions. Rather he can simply set up situations where the change would occur naturally: invite the person along on some activity, go out to dinner—the nonromantic equivalent of dating.

This is fine if the other person shares the interest in cultivating a friendship. But if you've seen the movie *The Cable Guy,* you might have an idea what it's like if the other person isn't interested.

Let's make this especially clear: if someone isn't interested in being your friend, lover, or wife, there is absolutely no way on earth to convince them they should. Don't try.

But... if the other person doesn't yet know how he or she feels about you, if you're someone they recognize but don't know, you can find out if there's interest. If the person doesn't know whether she's interested, you can explore the possibility. But if you think that someone who has already decided that your status as an acquaintance is just fine as far as she's concerned, read the paragraph above to yourself one more time—outloud.

Now, how do we go about helping our possible friend decide if he wants to be our definite friend? There's not much to it. Again, invite him along on some activity, something that he can do with you or you and your friends, or with another person you both know. If you've established a common interest, go with that.

The rules here are very similar to those of dating: if the person you're talking to is interested in the activity, he'll likely agree to go along if he's at all interested in spending time with you. If he says he's got other plans but would like to try it some other time, that's another indicator of possible interest. But if he quickly turns you down with no explanation or one designed to indicate that there's no interest (see the dating section), move on. You don't need to become a stalker.

Friendship is something that's especially hard to define, but you know it when you feel it. It helps us get through this lonely life with comfort, support, and enjoyment, and there is nothing more important to do on this planet.

While it's true that we choose our friends, our friends have to choose us, too. If they do, we're blessed. If they don't, we have to keep going and hope the next one does.

THE ABSOLUTE BASICS OF FRIENDSHIP

Be content to seem what you really are.

—MARTIAL

Okay, we've explored the phases of friendship and the reasons for friendship and the workings of friendship—in short, the theory of friendship. Now it's time to get to the nitty-gritty and discuss the nuts-and-bolts workings of friendship.

It's one thing to understand how to work through the difficult waters of an established friendship; it's another to know how long to keep a handshake going (three or four pumps). It's very important to know exactly how to cultivate a friendship with someone who shares an interest of yours, but it's equally important, in context, to know when to stop calling someone Mr. Walters and start calling him Jim.

So let's get a few basics of friendship (and just general courtesy) out in the open, and examine them. After all, knowing the proper way to start a conversation can be as important as finding a friend for life.

MEETING AND GREETING

Greetings vary not only from country to country, but in America from state to state. What's acceptable in France (the kiss on each cheek) would seem awfully odd in Iowa.

The acceptable form of greeting in America, for men and women, is the handshake. Embracing and kissing are acceptable for close friends and relatives, but handshakes are the proper greeting for everyone else. Clasp hands firmly (not crushing, not limp) and shake three or four times. And stand when you greet someone, a man or woman, unless you're physically incapable of doing so.

Make sure that you greet guests when you're hosting a party or other event—*all* your guests. If the doorbell rings and you're in a conversation, excuse yourself and go to the door. Everyone deserves a greeting.

Introductions

Once you've been introduced to someone, you are in a position to make the situation more comfortable for everyone. Start the conversation yourself unless there is one already in progress. People are generally a little tense in social situations and may feel awkward when a new person enters the conversation. If you start, you'll be taking the burden off everyone else.

By the way, when you're being introduced, make a point of letting people know what you like to be called. If someone introduces you as Robert, and you prefer Bob, you can shake hands and say, "Please, call me Bob." If someone introduces you as Robert and you like to be called Robert, simply let the introduction stand and say hello.

Just Talking

Conversation is an art, but you don't have to leave it to artists. Anybody can do it; it just takes a little practice. Try to find a common interest with the person you're talking with, and to begin, observe him or her. Is there a logo on his clothing that might indicate a certain interest (sports, an organization, a company—something)? Is she carrying a book or a magazine that might show something she's interested in (entertainment, exercise, cooking, rock climbing—anything)? Maybe you know something about that subject, too. If you don't, maybe you'd like to find out.

Think a little bit about the questions you ask. Try not to ask questions that can be answered with yes or no. Ask "why" questions instead of "what" questions, or "how" questions that might require an explanation. Not only does it get the conversation going, it also makes the person you're with feel like you're truly interested in him.

Avoid topics that the person might find too personal or distasteful. On first meeting, keep clear of any topic that might be offensive. Politics, religion, personal health, and sex are generally considered out of bounds for a first conversation.

Don't take the minister role too literally here—don't preach to people. Okay, so you're a recovering alcoholic, and she's having her third margarita. It's none of your business.

Listen. Let the person talk. Don't feel compelled to fill every pause with your own observation; let your new acquaintance take a breath.

Asking and Answering

There are personal questions that are acceptable between close friends, and unacceptable between people who don't know each other very well. These may include: "Have you lost weight?" "So how's the new boyfriend?" "Are you planning to have children?" and "What's going on with the tax audit?"

By the same token, some questions are just plain rude no matter how well you know the person you're asking. They are the questions you wouldn't want to answer yourself.

For example, *never* ask someone how old they are, if it's obvious they are over the age of nine. Kids are the only ones who find the question flattering, and even they might look miffed if you guess they are younger than they actually are. Adults, especially older adults, don't want to hear that question at all. If they want to discuss their age, believe me, they'll bring it up themselves.

Don't ask a woman with a prominent abdomen if she's pregnant. Sometimes they're not, and they're going to be very upset with you. Sometimes they are, and don't want to discuss it. In any case, it's just rude.

In fact, a friend tells me that when she was pregnant, strangers would stop her in public places and ask to rub her belly. She was appalled, and too shocked to come up with an answer. It is the absolute height of rudeness to do such a thing, and pregnant women shouldn't have to be subjected to that kind of behavior. Don't do it, and don't stand for it.

Some people ask expecting couples, "Is this a planned pregnancy?" I can't imagine anything more intimate than that, and can't believe anyone would have the nerve to say it outloud, but they do. Needless to say, this is not close to acceptable.

Questions about income levels, religion, political affiliation, and cosmetic surgery are also incredibly rude. Avoid these topics at all costs.

Other Questions to Avoid

Is that your natural hair color?
Remember me?
Did you get a raise recently?
Why aren't you drinking?
You got fired? What are you going to do now?

Care and Maintenance

Once a friendship is underway, it requires attention and maintenance, just like any other relationship. Contact must be maintained, which means that, like it or not, sooner or later, somebody is going to have to pick up the phone.

This seems to be the major stumbling block in many a friendship—who calls first. In fact, many friendships wither and die because one friend never picks up a phone, and the other gets tired of always having that responsibility. Sure, once the phone rings, both parties are happy to talk to each other and make plans for some activity together, but it becomes a serious problem that one person always has to initiate contact.

It is, in fact, quite inconsiderate to force your friend to call you every time there's going to be contact. It should, ideally, be a straight fifty-fifty sharing of responsibility, but you don't actually have to count, or be concerned with "whose turn it was last." The important thing is that both friends make an effort to call once in a while.

If you have a friend who seems never to call you, call your friend. But in this case, call to discuss how you feel about that. It's probably better to talk about it face-to-face, and use the Tiffany Theory to make the message more acceptable. It's not a huge problem, but it is one that can wreck a friendship over time.

Naturally, face-to-face contact is the best way to maintain a friendship, but sometimes that's just not possible. Sometimes friends live too far away from each other to get together on a regular basis; on occasion, jobs and families make such contact impossible. In any event, that doesn't mean this friendship is doomed.

It takes a little more effort, but you can keep contact with a friend when you're not seeing each other regularly. Still, there is an order to things: some modes of contact are, in fact, better than others. Here's a list, from best to worst, of the ways to keep up with a friend:

1. Regular, face-to-face meetings
2. Occasional face-to-face meetings, with phone calls in-between
3. Phone calls, from each friend to the other.
4. Notes and letters (newspaper clippings, etc.)
5. Fax (same material as in number 4, but less personal through technology)
6. E-mail (best for quick news updates, not in-depth thoughts)

7. A holiday card once a year

8. "Gee, I wonder what he's up to this decade…"

It should be noted, also, that there is a large drop-off in effectiveness and consideration between numbers 4 and 5 on the above list. A fax or an E-mail is just not as good as a handwritten note or letter.

Visits, or "Whose Turn Is It, Anyway?"

As with phone calls, visits or invitations to each other's home can become a point of contention with friends, especially new friends. Reciprocation is usually expected after one friend invites another over for dinner or a visit, and if it doesn't come, there can be friction.

In the beginning of a friendship, it's especially important to make sure that you haven't missed a turn, or failed to reciprocate for an invitation (except among cultures, like the Japanese, who reserve invitations for very close intimates). After years of friendship, it may become less important, but it may not, depending on the friends.

Be careful to make sure you do invite your friend back after being at her home for dinner. And while you may expect to have your invitation promptly returned, you'll be the one who has to decide whether the lack of an invitation is a sign of indifference, hostility, or simply the fact that your friend's apartment is too small to entertain (in which case, she should invite you out to dinner and pick up the check).

End of the Line

The best friendships last a lifetime—but not all friendships are the best. Sometimes, sadly, a friendship ends.

When a friendship dies, it's usually a slow, natural death. The time between phone calls or visits gets longer, interest on both sides seems to wane, and before either party notices, there hasn't been any contact in years. In a way, it's a blessing; it happened so slowly it was hard to notice.

The trouble comes when the death *isn't* slow and natural.

When there's a major disagreement and emotional scenes, the friendship can end acrimoniously and with great pain on both sides. It doesn't have to be that way, but it often is.

When a friendship ends this way and you're sure that it's over, not just going through a rough time, the only thing you can expect to do is to find out why. You are entitled to an explanation and required to give one if you're asked. Once again, the Tiffany Theory should be used, not to sugarcoat the facts or cover up the offense, but to help you to focus on the good times you've had, and remember why you were friends to begin with.

Yes, it's important to fight for a friendship that still has a chance of surviving; friends are among the most important people in our lives, and losing one will diminish our lives forever. But when the end is inevitable, it's best to be kind, fair, and humane. Let the friendship die, but let it die with dignity and grace.

THE FRIENDSHIP QUIZ

Answer each question honestly—no lying to yourself! Give yourself five points for each correct answer and add up the score at the end.

1. You're having an extramarital affair. Should you:
   a. tell your best friend?
   b. not tell anyone?
   c. tell only your friend who would be insulted if she *didn't* know?
   d. tell friends you can trust?

Answer: Actually, the real answer should be E, stop having an extramarital affair, but we didn't include that option. Out of the possibilities left, the best is probably B, but practicality will make C more likely. Give yourself two points for either of those.

2. You're getting married and your friend is starting to act strange, like she's being left out. You should:
   a. tell your soon-to-be spouse that your friend needs you, and include her in all your wedding plans.
   b. make your friend understand that your marriage is your top priority, and she's going to have to live with it.
   c. try to explain to your friend that things are changing.
   d. listen to your friend's concerns, and try to empathize.

Answer: This is a tricky one. It seems like D should be your answer, since it takes into account your friend's feelings, but B is actually the way to go. Your marriage is top priority and you have to protect it, but you have to explain that to your friend in your best Tiffany Theory manner.

3. Two of your friends are getting married, and you notice that they're not spending as much time with you as they used to. You:
    a. pout.
    b. assume your friends will now stop needing you and move on.
    c. have a heart-to-heart talk with your friends before the wedding.
    d. none of the above

Answer: D. These are all things you don't want to do yet. Writing off your friends is jumping the gun, since they haven't actually done anything except decide to marry. By the same token, having a deep conversation on the subject may be premature, too. These people haven't married yet; give them time to settle down. Wait and see. If things don't change, C will be the way to go, so give yourself two points for that, but five for D.

4. Your friends are already married, and they're having a serious argument. They each come to you separately for consolation and advice. You:
    a. do your Switzerland impression and remain neutral at all costs.
    b. listen to both sides and offer an honest opinion.
    c. side with the friend you've known longer.
    d. side with the friend of your gender (there's strength in solidarity).

Answer: A. You are not in place to be a marriage counselor, and taking sides in any case, no matter how clear the disagreement seems to you, will alienate one of your friends. Lend an ear, offer sympathy, but do not offer an opinion on who might be right. You want to keep both friends, don't you?

5. You've known your best friend for twenty years, and you can rely on him for anything. Lately, though, he's been acting a little aloof, and the phone hasn't rung in a while. You:
   a. assume he's busy and give him time.
   b. immediately call up and ask what his problem might be.
   c. call and invite him to dinner.
   d. send him a gift.

Answer: C. Confrontation isn't always necessary. Your friend might be suffering from a lack of attention. A dinner invitation will be just the thing to get the ball rolling—and don't take your friend for granted again!

6. You just met someone at a party and you've hit it off. You think you might want to spend some more time with this person, but you don't know her very well yet. You:
   a. suggest an activity you might both enjoy.
   b. ask a few well-hidden questions about sensitive subjects that mean a lot to you.
   c. be direct and ask about the make-or-break subjects.
   d. none of the above

Answer: A. You're not here to grill people and test them before you can make friends. There is no litmus test other than whether you enjoy each other's company, and the best way to determine that is to spend more time together and see if it's enjoyable.

7. You've made a new friend. You introduce her to your old friends, and it's clear they don't get along. Uh-oh. You:
   a. have to jettison your new friendship to protect the more important older ones.
   b. get upset with your old friends for being so inflexible, and spend more time with the new friend.
   c. try to get the two sides together again.
   d. spend time with each separately.

Answer: D. There's no sense in trying to get people who don't like each other to change their minds. You can choose your friends, but you can't choose *their* friends. So divide your time and keep all the friends you can rather than getting rid of one group to accommodate another. Life is too short.

8. You've become friendly with the parents of your son's best friend. Now your son and his friend have a big fight and don't want to see each other again. You:
   a. try to patch things up between the kids so you can keep your friends.
   b. make sure to remain neutral and talk to your friends about being neutral, too.
   c. protect your child and take his side.
   d. all of the above

Answer: B. Stay out of the kids' fight. You should have discussed this with your friends at the outset: What happens if the kids fight? Agree to stay out of the situation and keep your friendship separate from your children's. If the kids patch it up, fine; if they don't, you're entitled to keep your friends, anyway. And never discuss the details of the fight.

9. You've been friends for years, but you haven't gotten together in months. It doesn't feel like anything's wrong, but the friendship is clearly losing steam. You have to decide if it's worth saving. So, you:
   a. get mad because your friend is neglecting you.
   b. feel guilty because you're neglecting your friend.
   c. ask yourself if you really want to save the friendship.
   d. none of the above

Answer: C. The one test of a friendship is how you feel about it. If you really don't care whether you ever see this person again, the friendship has run its course and has died a natural death. If you do care, you have to take steps. Pick up the telephone and make a call.

10. You've called sixteen times in a row and gotten no calls in
    return. Now, every time you call, you have a good time
    with your friend, but she never calls to initiate the meeting.
    You:
    a. tell your friend this is a problem.
    b. keep calling to avoid damaging the friendship.
    c. assume this is your role in the relationship.
    d. all of the above

Answer: A. But use the Tiffany Theory.

11. You've known someone very casually for a while and
    decide you'd like to know him better. You ask him to join
    you for rock climbing, but he declines. You:
    a. ask him out to dinner.
    b. refuse to take no for an answer.
    c. find another interest.
    d. give up.

Answer: Believe it or not, D. You don't want to become a
stalker. If someone's truly not interested in making the relationship more intimate, let it go. You can't change someone's mind
if they're not interested.

12. You're at a party, and a woman is introduced to you as Ms.
    Waldner. You address her as:
    a. Ms. Waldner.
    b. Gloria (someone told you her first name).
    c. Mrs. Waldner.
    d. it doesn't matter.

Answer: A. If the person in question doesn't make a point of
saying what she likes to be called, go with the introduction.
Exactly. "Sweetie" is not acceptable.

13. You've stumbled into a conversation at a party with
    someone you've never met, and there is an extremely
    awkward silence. You:

    a.   wait for the other person to start a conversation so you'll know what she's interested in discussing.

    b.   start the conversation yourself.

    c.   try to get someone else involved.

    d.   none of the above

Answer: B. Start it up yourself. The other person will be grateful to you, and you'll be discussing a topic in which you have at least some interest. Maybe you'll make a new friend.

14. Your conversation isn't going well; you're getting nothing but one-word answers from your partner. The next word you say should be:

    a.   I

    b.   you

    c.   what

    d.   how

Answer: D. Asking a question that begins with "how" or "why" will ensure that you can't get an answer consisting of yes or no. The other person will have to go further to explain himself. If the "how" or "why" question deals with something you believe he has an interest in, you may have started an actual conversation.

15. Someone you barely know walks up to you in a social situation and asks, "Did I hear that you just got a big raise?" You:

    a.   try to deflect the question with humor: "I don't know; did you hear that?"

    b.   smile and change the topic.

    c.   calmly state that this isn't the place for such a question.

    d.   any of the above

Answer: D. This is an unspeakably rude question and doesn't deserve an answer. You're not required to provide that kind of information in such an informal setting.

16. Your friendship has ended, and it's obvious to everyone except your friend. When she demands an explanation, you:

   a. brush up on your Tiffany Theory.
   b. simply state that things have run their course.
   c. refuse to give one.
   d. none of the above

Answer: A. Even an ex-friend deserves an explanation. Wrap it in your best Tiffany paper, but be firm if you're certain that this relationship is over. Friendships usually die a natural death (if they die at all), but some need to be put out of their misery.

Score

   0–15: You don't get out much, do you?
  16–30: Hold on tight to the friends you have.
  31–50: Doing well, but room for improvement.
  51–65: You're a good friend.
  66–77: Maybe you should write your own book.

7

Losses

WHEN BAD THINGS HAPPEN TO ANYONE

Men die but an idea does not.

—ALAN JAY LERNER

Life, it should be noted, ain't fair. Bad things happen to good people; they also happen to bad people. People lose jobs; people lose money; people have their dreams taken away. They get sick, sometimes seriously ill. People die. Sometimes they are the people we love. Those of us who are left behind after a death, or are here with those who must cope with a tragedy, need to use our healer roles more than anyone else. But sometimes healing means letting our loved ones feel the pain.

"We try to minimize grief," writes Crystal Gromer in a *Vogue* essay on her husband, Mark's, untimely death and the reactions of those around her. "'At least he didn't suffer,' people say. 'At least he's not a vegetable.' Any time you hear 'at least' come out of your mouth, stop. Creating an imaginary worse scenario doesn't make the real and current one better. It trivializes it. 'At least you're young,' people said to me. 'At least you have your life ahead of you.' *What? So this doesn't count?* Hearing that I had my life ahead of me only reminded me that I had to slog through perhaps fifty years without Mark. The rest of us need to acknowledge the importance of grief and let it be, not try to make it disappear."

Crystal Gromer's words explain beautifully why it's important to have rules for behavior—that is, etiquette—when dealing with those who are grieving or experiencing hardship. If we don't know what to do or say—and those are often the first words we hear from those who try to help: "I don't know what to say"—then nothing can help as much as etiquette. Not having to improvise in the most awkward and difficult situation of all is a blessing.

Of course, grief and tragedy are not one awkward situation. Hardship befalls each of us at some time or another, often more than once, sometimes simultaneously. The way we deal with someone else's grief may have something to do with the way we wanted others to deal with ours in the past, or the way we imagine we would like them to deal with it should we have to face tragedy in the future. The rule of doing to others as we would have them do to us is never more appropriate.

So, what *should* we do when we have to console a loved one? How do we deal with the loss of someone we loved, the loss of a job or the loss of one's health? How do we deal with it when someone close to us loses any of those things? What are the rules, and how can we apply them?

Here are a few examples of awkward situations:

Your friend, whom you've known for twenty-five years, loses her husband. What can you possibly say to ease her pain?

Your company is downsizing and your job is safe, but your friend's is being eliminated.

Your uncle passes away, and your aunt is inconsolable. You hear that she's asking for contributions to a certain charity in lieu of flowers or food, but you don't know how to get in touch with the charity, and you don't want to disturb your aunt with a question like that right now.

Your boss dies. You never liked him, but all employees are expected to attend the funeral. What do you say to his wife?

You lose your wife after fifteen years of marriage, and people keep telling you to "get back out there" as soon as you can. You find what they say is in absolutely awful taste, and you want to tell them that. Should you?

Your friend of another faith passes away, and you're going to attend the service, but you've never been in a church of this denomination before. What do you need to know ahead of time?

Your sister loses her husband. You know what *not* to say, but what *should* you say?

Keep reading. It's all here.

LOSING LOVED ONES

Tell me what to do/When the light of my life is gone from me/There's a smile on my face/But I'm only pretending.

—THE ALAN PARSONS PROJECT, from Hellyrres to "Same Old Sun," written by Alan Parsons and Eric Woolfson

There is nothing worse than losing a loved one. Nothing. Death takes all our loved ones from us, eventually, and our sheer powerlessness in its face is overwhelming. The only thing we can do is cope the best we can, and continue on.

For people who have experienced a loss, there is ritual and there is comfort from those who care. Ritual serves its purpose, and depending on your faith, it comes before or after the lost loved one is laid to rest, and can last a day or two or a week or more. It can consist of raucous remembrances or solemn contemplation. The key to ritual is that whichever one best suits your faith and your temperament is the one to observe. There are reasons for each of the steps along the way, and even if some of those reasons have been lost to time, the repetition and inevitability of those reasons hold comfort for some people.

Comfort from those who have been left behind is more random. It can appear in the form of unspoken, sensitive support, or it can be clumsy, awkward demonstrations of emotion and the wrong words at the wrong time. That's where a strong Social I.Q. is especially handy.

First of all, there is nothing wrong with expressing grief. It's a natural emotion, and there is good reason for it. What *is* wrong is expressing grief to the person who has experienced the loss—the spouse, child or parent of the deceased. They have enough to feel sad about, and this moment is not about you and your feelings—it's about them. People need for you to acknowledge that they have suffered a terrible loss and that you sympathize. They do not need to hear that you have suffered a terrible loss and that they should sympathize. That emotion is for you to express outside their earshot.

The flip side of that advice is to avoid the artificial chipper, jocular tone that some feel best masks the raw sadness of grief. Planting a phony smile on your face and making a half-hearted joke aren't going to help. Be honest but supportive, and not self-centered.

"After Mark died," Crystal Gromer writes, "I felt as if people saw me as a tragic heroine. People tended to look at their hands when they talked to me...I felt lonely, a self no one wanted to know."

What words are the right ones to say to someone who is grieving?

Usually, what people would like to hear are happy memories of the lost loved one. Explain to the widow what her husband meant to you through an especially telling anecdote, one that has a happy ending.

Offering such stories might seem like an exercise in bad taste, but it is exactly the opposite. You're not rubbing the bereaved person's nose in the fact that they've lost a loved one; you're reminding that person exactly why their loved one was so special to begin with. Good memories are, after all, our only lasting possessions, and they are to be kept as close to our hearts as possible.

"Preserve your memories," sang Simon and Garfunkel. "They're all that's left you."

Sometimes people feel awkward about sharing their memories with a grieving spouse or child because they want to avoid reminding their relative or friend of the loss. It's understandable to be concerned about that, but it's still best to use the remembrance. Yes, it may hurt to hear an especially endearing story, but it will certainly help to have the perspective that the story provides. The thought that their loved one's life touched so many others is great comfort to many mourners. Don't deprive them of that feeling.

It is also important to send a card of condolence as soon as you hear about a death. Avoid terms like "words can't express my feelings" or "I know there's nothing that can help," because they *don't* help, and you're already using words to try to express your feelings. Instead, concentrate on expressing support, and if you're not going to attend the funeral or visit before or after the ceremony, this might be a good opportunity to share the memory you would like to express. Do it as clearly as you can, and explain why it's special for you.

Some people wait too long after a death to send a note or card, and then tell themselves that they shouldn't resurrect another's grief a week, a month, or six months later. This is cowardly and unfair. Go ahead and send the card whenever you can. Of course, it's better to do it as soon as you can, but tardiness is no excuse. This person will be living with the loss for the rest of his or her life. Anytime is appropriate.

Sending flowers or food is also appropriate in many cases, but it depends on the religion of the family involved. Most Christian faiths, for example, favor flowers at a funeral, while Jews, except Reform Jews, generally forsake flowers and ask for contributions to charity or food sent to the home of the mourners. Your best bet is to call the funeral home (which is listed in a newspaper's death notices) and ask what is appropriate to send and where to send it.

The funeral itself will also vary from religion to religion. The wake, or a gathering before the funeral to comfort the bereaved and gather to mark the passing, is a Christian tradition. Jews will "sit shiva," or gather in the home of one of the mourners, but only after the funeral, and usually for about a week. Other faiths' traditions will vary, and as soon as you hear of the death it's best to check with the funeral home to ask about schedules and traditions. The church, synagogue, mosque, or other house of faith will also be able to answer your questions regarding specific customs.

In any event, attending the funeral is certainly expected of relatives and close friends. Acquaintances have the option of attending or simply sending a note or a token (flowers, food) and calling later to offer support. If you attend the funeral, you have to wear somber clothing to show respect for the dead and those who are mourning. The mourners may be available before the ceremony to receive guests. If you have attended a wake or plan on visiting after the ceremony, don't tell the mourners your special memory at this time. They have enough on their minds right now. Wait until they have more time to think and appreciate what you're saying.

The funeral itself is a time for religious customs and family members, and perhaps a few very close friends, who will offer eulogies and memories of the deceased. If you are called upon to deliver a eulogy, think both of the deceased person and what he would have wanted to hear, and the mourners, who will actually hear it. Keep your remarks short and to the point, and try to keep them positive. Try not to become too emotional during your speech.

Only close relatives and very close friends are expected to attend the interment, unless the funeral service is being held at graveside. If you decide to attend, try to find out the appropriate customs and rites for the religion involved ahead of time. There are, believe it or not, web sites that will help (use your search engine) and books, like *How to Be a Perfect Stranger,* edited by Arthur J. Magida (Jewish Lights Publishing), which list the appropriate way to act while attending many religious ceremonies.

Death is not something that we are meant to take lightly, nor is it something we can ignore. It touches all of us at one point or another in our lives, and we have to prepare ahead of time to deal with it. When you are called upon to confront death, to support someone else whose life it has irreparably harmed, arm yourself with a strong Social I.Q. It will get you through the hard times and help you support someone who needs you. It is the strongest example of the value of Social I.Q.: Through your use of the proper rules and the ability to minister and heal, you can spread ripples of calm across a sea of sadness and make at least a small part of the world a better place for your fellow human beings.

When You Are the Mourner

There's no easy way to get through grief. In fact, there's no hard way to get through it, either. It eases, you get used to it, but it never truly goes away. The person you have lost will be a loss in your life forever, and it is, perhaps, a mistake of our culture that we expect all things to heal, that we think "time heals all wounds." Time *doesn't* heal all wounds. It just places layer after layer of scar tissue over them. Pull off the scab, and the wound is still visible. And it still hurts.

If you have experienced the loss of a loved one, you know how it feels. You also know that other people don't know exactly how your loss feels, and that they will often say or do the wrong things, even when they're trying to offer you support and empathy. It doesn't help that their intentions are good; it only hurts when they say something that emphasizes, rather than eases, your grief.

The problem is, you can't lash out at them. For one thing, it would be inappropriate, since the person is trying to help, however clumsily. For another, it wouldn't do any good, since the person probably wouldn't understand what is upsetting you, and would assume that grief has simply gotten the best of you. He might even be right about that.

People who lose a spouse often report the most insensitive remarks regarding their future romantic relationships directed at them: "You should get right out there and start dating again" is not unusual. And nothing could be more unfeeling and inappropriate.

Reacting to such a remark takes a considerable amount of tact, something the bereaved might have in short supply. It might just be best to ignore the remark, but if you feel you have to react, don't give in to your impulse to scream. Simply say you don't think you want to consider that after so recent a loss, and thank the person for his concern.

What you can do is control the situation as tightly as is possible. Obviously, the loss of a loved one is something entirely out of your hands, but the way the loss is handled, the way it is observed, is something that is within your control. Exercise that control; it will give you something on which to concentrate, and you can avoid some of the more awkward moments that might be on the horizon by anticipating them and creating circumstances that will stop them before they can start. For example:

Make sure the published death notices list the time and place of the funeral.

Give the funeral home specific directions to your home (if people are going to be gathering there) or to the cemetery. Let people ask the home for directions so they don't have to bother you.

Make sure any information about suggested charitable donations is included in the death notice (which is separate from an obituary, by the way; death notices are the small-type boxes that appear on the same page).

Ask someone outside the nuclear family (a close friend, a relative) to call relatives and friends to advise them of the death. You don't have to do it yourself.

Look people in the eye when they approach you; it might give them the signal that you wish to be looked in the eye too.

Stimulate their memories by sharing one of your own which involves them: "You know, my dad always said you were a great poker player."

Don't be afraid to express your emotions. This is your time

to grieve, and grieving is a natural, healing thing. Don't let other people's perceptions keep you from helping yourself. You're the one who needs help now, not them.

If your religion is a comfort to you, conform to all its rituals and rites. If some customs bother you and you are not especially observant, indulge in the ones that comfort you and ignore the rest. Religion is something that should be there for your support, not to torment you.

Accept offers of condolence with a heartfelt thank you, and don't expect other people to know what you're thinking. Tell them what you need.

If someone says something inappropriate—for example, telling a grieving widow to "get back out there and start dating soon"—don't respond to it. Starting an argument at this point would be counterproductive, and someone that insensitive is probably beyond help anyway.

Give yourself permission to grieve. You're *supposed to* feel bad. Gather strength from it, and keep going. There's no excuse for giving up.

THE RULES OF MOURNING

It would be unbearable if memory didn't exist... I hear your laughter. I see you writing in your office... At will, I can spend hours with you.

—JEANNE MOREAU on the death of her best friend, Francois Truffaut

A few subjects involving the mourning process:

Notifying Loved Ones

One person (usually a friend or relative, but not a member of the immediate family) should be designated to call all those who need to be notified of the death. Petty family differences must be overlooked; this is a larger issue.

Another family member or friend should be given the responsibility to answer the phone at the bereaved family's home. Widows and children of the deceased are not expected to fulfill this responsibility, and it is not at all rude to screen calls for people whose lives have undergone so violent an upheaval. The people who have suffered the loss get to decide with whom they wish to speak right now, and the decisions should not be questioned.

To Tell or Not to Tell

It is very rare that a relative is told about a death only after the funeral. The only times this is appropriate are when the relative is absolutely unreachable within a reasonable amount of time (Jewish funerals, for example, take place as quickly as possible after the death, and there isn't always time to find relatives who are out of the country), or when the relative in question is very elderly or so frail that she couldn't stand the shock. But it is a very ticklish issue, and in almost all cases the proper thing to do is to notify the relative in question.

Funeral Plans

Plans for the service, memorial, and burial or cremation are the responsibility of the next of kin: a spouse, if one is living; children, if no parent is alive; parents, if a child is the deceased. If the person who has died is unmarried and has no children or parents, a sibling would be the next of kin.

The next of kin plans the service, decides on the casket, and chooses the clothes in which the loved one will be buried or cremated. Some religions prefer a shroud, but in America most people opt to bury their loved ones in slightly formal clothes— men in suits, women in suits or dresses. Music is also selected by the next of kin, unless the deceased left specific instructions ahead of time.

If you want to speak at the funeral, let the funeral director know ahead of time. The funeral director will speak to the deceased person's family and will let you know whether you'll be allowed to speak. The decision of the family is final.

If you have been selected as a pallbearer, the family or the funeral director will notify you before the service. If you feel that you're not able to perform that duty, let the funeral director or family know immediately so they can find a substitute.

Ex-spouses

This is no time for a divorce to be relived. If an ex-spouse wishes to attend the funeral, there should be no question. Still, the ex, if there has been difficulty between himself and the family or the new spouse, should keep a respectful distance from the mourners.

Suicide

In the case of a person taking his own life, the cause of death is often not discussed. Many newspapers will not disclose the cause when suicide is involved, and sometimes will refer to a "sudden illness" instead. In any case, it is not helpful to ask everyone at the funeral what happened, or to refer to "the accident" when it's clear that no accident occurred. Simply treat the death as any other and move on. Gossip at a funeral is absolutely intolerable.

Death Notices and Obituaries

As part of the responsibility for notifying anyone who might have an interest in attending the funeral, the next of kin should instruct the funeral director to place death notices and obituaries in certain newspapers. The publications will usually include the hometown paper of the person's most recent residence, as well as newspapers where he or she might have spent a significant portion of his or her life.

A death notice is a small box, usually starting with the deceased's last name and a dash. The information contained in the box is very specific regarding any services that will be conducted on behalf of the deceased, the address of the funeral home, and where and when interment will take place if there is to be interment.

An obituary is a longer, more prominent short newspaper article that reports the death, but also talks about the life of the person who has passed on. It will run in the newspaper depending on the space allotted for obituaries in that day's edition and the notoriety of the deceased. The funeral director supplies the information, but the newspaper makes the publication decision. Death notices, on the other hand, are paid for (and are usually included in the funeral home's fee) and will run when the mourners want them to run.

Guest Book

A guest book will be present at the funeral parlor, and often in the home of the mourners when guests are being received there. It is a good idea to sign the guest book, because bereaved relatives are often in something of a fog and may not clearly remember everyone who drops by. Sign with whatever name you prefer to have on a thank you note.

Condolence Cards

Store-bought cards are fine, but don't simply sign your name; put in a handwritten note, preferably one with a short memory of the deceased. (See template, page 246) In any event, try to avoid terms like "words can't express my sorrow" in favor of "my thoughts ('prayers,' if you are religious) are with you."

Thank You Cards

If you are the grieving family member, the funeral director will supply you with preprinted acknowledgments that you can send to family and friends who sign the guest book. These are also helpful to send to those who send flowers, food, or notes.

It is unacceptable, however, to send a preprinted card to close family or friends without a handwritten note that adds your own thoughts. If the grieving family is truly unable to send notes, this can be done by a close family member in their name, but it is usually better for the family to send the notes themselves.

Pallbearers

These should be selected from among the deceased's closest family and friends. Usually six pallbearers are chosen, but more can be added as "ceremonial" pallbearers, particularly for those physically incapable of lifting the casket from the cart into the hearse and out again. Sometimes the deceased will have left instructions. Otherwise, the next of kin will make the decision, based on what she thinks the deceased would have wanted. Again, this is no time for petty differences to get in the way.

Children at Funerals

You know your child best. If he or she can handle the ceremony and will not cause a disruption, it is appropriate to bring your child along. But if you honestly believe your child will be seriously disturbed or will not be able to sit through the service quietly, do your child, the assembled, and yourself a favor and arrange for a baby-sitter at home.

Funeral for a Nonfriend

Here's a tricky one—your boss dies, and employees are expected to attend the funeral. But you never liked him, and you know that nobody else in the company did either. He was a mean old guy, and you're not the least bit sorry he's dead.

Still, to protect your job and to be polite, you attend the funeral. His wife, obviously distraught, is receiving guests, and you're approaching her. What should you say?

If you don't have a happy memory of the man, you simply take her hand and tell her you're sorry she's experienced such a loss. It's not necessary to lie, and it's not necessary to tell her that you didn't like her late husband. All you have to do to be polite is acknowledge her pain, which is clearly real, and sympathize with it. It's not hypocrisy to act as a healer for someone who has suffered a loss, no matter how little the loss might mean to you.

WHEN SOMEONE YOU LOVE FALLS ILL

You don't get to choose how you're going to die. Or when. You can only decide how you're going to live.

—JOAN BAEZ, "Daybreak"

Illness can be a devastating, draining experience for people who are not at all sick. If you have been close to someone who has survived a bout with cancer or is living through another debilitating illness, you know that much has been written about the emotional cost the patient pays. But you know just as well that the patient's family and his friends pay just as high a cost, sometimes over a period of months or years.

It can sometimes feel in your heart like the patient gets the better end of the deal, even though your brain knows her suffering is more awful than yours. Some people living with chronic patients, with long-term illnesses, can begin to resent the sick person, however subconsciously, for all the suffering that's happening around them.

In short, it's hard to be the patient, and it's hard to watch someone you love—a spouse, child, parent, family member, or friend—fall seriously ill. Fear of death and the pain of seeing a loved one who is sick can combine to drain the joy out of anyone who comes in contact with the patient. As much as Social I.Q. dictates that the phrase "at least his suffering is over" is wrong when a loved one dies, we can understand where the sentiment originates. What is really meant is: "At least *my* suffering, due to this illness, has ended." Of course, the suffering of loss is just beginning.

So, what is the right thing to do in this terribly awkward situation, and one that most people would do almost anything to avoid? Luckily, there is etiquette.

When you find out that someone in your family or a close friend is ill, call right away. You may not get the patient on the phone, but someone staying with him will answer.

Offer to help. You can ask what needs to be done, but make your offer tangible—offer to do something specific, even if it's doing the marketing or picking up the dry cleaning.

Maintain contact. If visits are being allowed, by all means drop by. If they're not, this is one of the rare instances in which E-mail and faxes are better than a phone call and faster than a note. Use technology to its best advantage.

When you visit, don't spend all your time talking about the illness. Let the patient, if she's well enough, direct the conversation into the topics she wants to discuss. Otherwise, stick to the cheerful, but don't be so artificially sweet that she'll be even sicker when you leave.

Keep the visit short. Sick people need rest, even if they don't think so. Come often, but leave early.

Yes, bring a gift. It doesn't have to be anything big and expensive, and you don't have to do this every time if you're going to visit frequently, but do bring something at least the first time you come.

Bring a video. Watching it is something that you can do together, and can be done indoors, with a minimum of physical exertion. And it's best to make it a comedy or a musical.

Check before you bring food. There may be restrictions on the patient's diet. The last thing you want to do is to arrive with something your friend can't eat.

Send E-mail when you can't visit. It's the easiest way to get a message with a minimum of effort on the recipient's part. If the patient doesn't have a computer, send a fax. If he doesn't have a fax, send a telegram. It's faster than a letter, and raising an ill person's spirits quickly is the goal.

Take some breaks. You don't have to devote every minute of your life to another person's illness. Maintain your sanity.

If the illness drags on for a long time, it's going to be difficult to maintain your stamina. Keep sending notes, keep calling, but don't feel guilty if you miss a day. Just make sure you give some notice when you have to cancel a visit. Don't leave a sick friend expecting a visit that won't come.

There's nothing pleasant about a long or severe illness, but with a strong Social I.Q. you can make the experience less difficult for someone close to you—and that is, without question, the aim of anyone with *any* kind of I.Q.

WHEN YOU ARE ILL

> *Most men think they are immortal—until they get a cold, when they think they are going to die within the hour.*
>
> —NORMAN COUSINS, *Human Options*

It's one thing to have a cold; it's something else entirely to be very ill. It's one thing to help take care of a sick person; it's something else entirely to actually *be* that sick person.

There's something that has to be said right up front: nobody likes to be sick, and nobody likes to be around sick people. It's natural, and it's understandable. But it's also sometimes unavoidable, and there's nothing you can do in a situation like that but to make the best of it.

You can be relatively sure that if you become ill, people will visit, and you can be just as sure that some of them—the ones who haven't read this book—will say the wrong thing.

Your first job as a patient is to get well. Whatever it takes, you have to regain your health. Put your energy, thoughts, and actions into that goal. It's your full-time job.

Beyond that, you have a few other responsibilities. Keeping in mind that you *are* going to get well, you're probably going to want to have some friends when you're back on your feet.

Toward that end, this is the time to maintain those friendships. Mostly, you do that by overlooking some of the less sensitive comments made in your presence. You overlook the people who talk about you as if you're not there. You overlook the people who bring food you can't eat, gifts you can't use, and nothing at all. You overlook—period.

What are your responsibilities as a patient? There are very few, but a few:

Have someone let those close to you know about your illness—as much as you're comfortable having them know.

Try to welcome guests when they arrive, and do your best not to dwell on your medical condition.

Be honest. If you're not able to see anyone, have someone call and cancel visits if you're not physically up to it.

Send thank you notes for gifts or visits if you can. If you can't, either have someone else to do so, or send E-mail or faxes. Call on the phone if you can.

If someone comes in and gasps at how awful you look, makes an insensitive remark, or makes a point of calling instead of visiting, and you want to keep the friendship alive, you have to overlook the insult.

Do all you can to improve your condition—it's what everyone wants.

LOSING A JOB

Anything that begins, "I don't know how to tell you this," is never good news.

—Ruth Gordon

A survey taken in the 1980s showed that after the death of a loved one, being fired was the most traumatic event that could occur to anyone. It is a possibility for virtually everyone (except the self-employed, and their business is always subject to the market), and can happen at any time. It can mean radical changes to any life, the lives of the family involved, and the lives of coworkers. None of these changes are good ones.

Being fired, beyond the fact of no longer having an income or a place to report for work every day, has implications in any worker's life. Coworkers who are considered friends will not be a part of the daily routine anymore. There's the drop in self-esteem that accompanies a firing, even when the company is downsizing. There can be panic. Sometimes there can be depression or despair.

There is a period of mourning the loss of a job, just as there is a similar period after the death of a friend or a loved one. The feeling usually isn't as intense, and the period will hopefully be shorter, but it exists, and it has to be observed and allowed.

In the film *Kramer vs. Kramer,* there's a sequence in which Dustin Hoffman, playing an advertising executive facing a bitter custody battle for his son, is fired from his job. Knowing that this will affect his chances to keep his son in his home, Hoffman's character frantically goes from agency to agency, trying to find employoment. He ends up taking a serious pay cut and practically begging for a job at an agency during its company Christmas party.

That sequence illustrates the feelings that follow being fired. First, there is the realization that dire consequences can result from this event. Panic sets in. But there's also a determination which surfaces to find something new, and the excitement of knowing that the "something new" could be *anything*. You are no longer bound by any constraints. That's the area on which to focus.

There's nothing like losing a job to open up possibilities, but you have to be ready for them. By the same token, there's nothing like a firing to bring out the pettiness in coworkers and awkward behavior in friends and family.

First, think about why you were fired. It's going to make a difference when you look for another job. If it was your performance, you're going to have to take a long, serious look at yourself and your attitude toward work. If it was a case of corporate downsizing, or a layoff due to poor conditions for the whole company, you will be more easily able to market yourself to a new company.

Ask your supervisor if you can use the company as a reference when you look for a new job. In fact, ask your former employer for a letter of reference, and if she agrees, use it to find new work. Of course, your old boss might not want you to see the letter she writes, in which case you might want to be careful about offering it. If she says, "Just ask the company you're applying to if they want to contact me," you might want to think twice about using her as a reference. If she says, "Sure, here's a letter of recommendation," read the letter, thank your ex-boss, and use it (assuming it says complimentary things about your performance).

Dealing with the emotional side of the loss is as difficult—if not more so—than the practical, financial loss. If someone you know is fired, it is extremely thoughtless to approach him with a greeting like, "My god, you were fired, what are you going to do *now?*" It is much more appropriate to say, "Is there anything I can do to help?" or "Where are you going to start looking?" Accentuate the positive, which does *not* mean "That job was no good for you, anyway," but does mean, "You're good enough to get something new very quickly."

There is bound to be a period during which the firing victim indulges his anger. Some actually plot to get even with the employer, and write long, emotional letters to "give him a piece of my mind." There's nothing wrong with writing these letters. What's wrong is mailing them. Get all the anger off your chest and onto paper, then quickly tear it up and throw it away. Burn it, if it makes you feel better. Do *something,* but don't actually send that letter under any circumstances. If you're with a friend who's been fired and she writes such a letter and won't be dissuaded, offer to mail it for her—and throw it away on the way home.

You've heard the adage that an optimist sees the glass half full while the pessimist sees the same glass half empty. There are also two ways of looking at having lost your job: either you can see it as the ending of your current career or the beginning of a new one. If you believe the world has endless possibilities, you'll have a much better attitude and a better chance of starting a new job soon.

Nobody says it will be easy, and nobody says you should enjoy it, but you do have to go out and find another job before the bills come due. As the writer J. Chalmers Da Costa once said, "It won't help a young man much to be one hundred years ahead of his time if he is a month behind in his rent."

Consider another possibility: Your job is secure, but your friend, who works on the other side of your cubicle wall, has been downsized. There's bound to be some resentment, but you still want to console him. What can you possibly say?

You can't hide, and you can't ignore the fact that you're still an employee and he's not. Say things like, "I'm so sorry this happened to you," but not "I wish it had been me instead," because you don't wish it had been you instead, and your friend knows that.

Take your friend out for a drink or dinner after the firing, and tell him you'll support him emotionally as well as you can. Don't offer money unless you can truly afford it and know he'll need it badly. Suggest places for him to look for a new job. Don't spend the next few weeks calling him with office gossip; he's gone now, and you don't want to remind him that you're still there. If he wants to see his old friends from the office, help him organize it, but let him suggest it first.

Above all, be supportive. You're a healer and a minister. Listen and empathize, and then listen and empathize some more. Expect anger, even if it's unexpressed. Think how you would feel if the situation were reversed, and overlook all that you can. Sooner or later, your friend will find another job, but you don't want him to lose a friend.

DOING THE FIRING

A man feared that he might find an assassin; another that he might find a victim. One was more wise than the other.

—STEPHEN CRANE, "The Black Riders"

It's possible, although unlikely, that it's harder to fire an employee than to be the employee being fired. Well, maybe not. But it's not a great joy, either.

Still, there are times when firing is necessary, and somebody has to do it. If you are the immediate supervisor of the employee in question, you are likely to be the one chosen to do the job, and no matter what the circumstances, you're going to have to do it.

So, how do you go about doing it and maintain your Social I.Q.?

First, give a warning before a firing is necessary. If an employee's performance has not been what it should be or there is some other problem, the employee should have the right to try to improve the situation before being fired. Call the employee in, shut the door, and explain precisely what the problem appears to be. Detail clearly what needs to be done to improve the situation, and set out a specific amount of time—two weeks, a month, two months on the outside—after which the employee's performance will be evaluated again. Make it clear that if there is no improvement, firing is the next step.

Second, try to help the employee improve. Maybe this firing can be avoided.

Third, if the employee has not improved his performance in the specified amount of time, call him in again. Shut the door. For legal reasons, you might want to have witnesses present. It is very important that you remain calm, no matter how the employee acts. If the scene gets truly ugly, you might want to have company security personnel nearby to escort the employee out of the building.

Some employers prefer to fire people late in the business day on a Friday, to allow the entire company to recover from the incident over the weekend. Others feel it's best to do the firing as soon as possible after the decision to do so has been made. Clearly, this will be your decision, but the key will be to do the firing in as civilized and calm a manner as you possibly can.

If possible, have a printed list of the employee's benefits and severance package available when you do the firing. Letting someone go is an emotional experience for both of you, and the employee might not remember everything that's being said. The more information you can have on paper to hand over, that can be taken home, the better off you will be.

Severence packages vary from company to company. It is routine to give an employee two weeks notice from the time he is fired until the time he must leave the company. This may not be possible if the employee is being fired "for cause," that is, if there is a serious, ongoing problem like drug abuse, alcoholism, or mental instability involved.

In cases of downsizing or layoffs, you may be firing an employee based on company concerns and not the employee's performance. In these cases, you might want to offer a written recommendation, or offer to recommend the employee to other prospective employers who call. Give him permission to use your name when offering references, or write a letter of recommendation and hand it to him before he leaves. When the employee is being fired for other reasons, of course, you might not want to recommend him, and if he asks you for a reference when he's being fired, you should tactfully tell him that you don't think it would be appropriate.

Sometimes, private employees are fired, that is, people whom you employ privately—nannies, housekeepers, gardeners, and maids—have to be let go. The procedure is roughly the same, although without the corporate layers of bureaucracy. Give the warning, evaluate the performance, and if things don't improve, do the firing.

Nobody likes being fired, and few employers like doing the firing. But business being business, it is sometimes necessary.

Social I.Q. demands that you treat someone as you would like to be treated yourself, but circumstances have to be taken into account. Obviously, you wouldn't want anyone to fire you, but if you had to be fired, how would you want it to be done? That is the question you must answer before calling the employee into your office—and shutting the door.

THE LOSSES QUIZ

Answer each question honestly. Five points for each correct answer.

1. You've lost your father after a long illness, and at the wake, a business associate—whom you barely know—embraces you and begins wailing loudly about the loss she's suffered. You:
   a. begin to weep too, to show how bereaved you are.
   b. pat her gently and try to move her to another business friend whom she knows better.
   c. whisper to her that this is inappropriate and ask her to stop.
   d. none of the above

Answer: B. It's a close call, since this isn't the most sensitive thing in the whole world to do, but this woman is acting inappropriately. You are a mourner, and she shouldn't be assuming the evening is about *her* grief. Give yourself two points if you answered D.

2. You're going to see a friend who has lost her husband. You know you don't want to depress her further, so the minute you see her, you:
   a. tell her a joke.
   b. hug her tightly and say nothing.
   c. launch into a happy memory of her husband.
   d. none of the above

Answer: D. I know you think it should be C, but the key

words here are "the minute you see her." This is not something with which you can assault a person in mourning. Find a time to remember something special, but not immediately on entering the room.

3. So what should you do?
   a. Wait until you are alone and share the memory.
   b. Hold her tightly, say you're there if she needs you, and move on.
   c. Offer support and look her in the eye when you do it.
   d. all of the above

Answer: D, again. These are all things that are appropriate to do in these circumstances. Two points if you answered with any one of them.

4. You've heard about a friend losing her brother, but it's been two weeks and you haven't sent a card. It's now inappropriate to simply send a card. True or false?

Answer: False. Passing time is no excuse. Send the card and include a handwritten note in it.

5. A cousin has died, and you hear from your mother that the family is asking for donations to a charity in lieu of flowers. But your mother didn't get the name of the charity. You:
   a. call the mourners' home and ask.
   b. check the death notice.
   c. check the obituary.
   d. all of the above

Answer: B. The information is more likely to be included in the death notice—the small box on the obituary page—than in the obituary. Calling the mourners for this information at this time would be in bad taste.

6. Your spouse has passed away, and the phone has already started ringing. You:
   a. ask a friend or relative to answer and screen all calls.
   b. answer the phone yourself.
   c. ask one of your children to answer the phone.
   d. none of the above

Answer: A. If no one volunteers, it's perfectly appropriate to ask for help with the phone. Someone should also be calling relatives and friends with the news, and it shouldn't be you or anyone in your immediate family.

7. Your mother has passed away, and your uncle, who is ninety-eight years old, might not be able to stand the news. You:
   a. tell him anyway.
   b. conceal the information from him.
   c. consult his doctor.
   d. It depends.

Answer: D. No answer is always right in this circumstance. Give yourself two points for A, since, in most cases, withholding the information of a loved one's passing is unacceptable.

8. Your late wife's ex-husband wants to attend her funeral. This is:
   a. inappropriate.
   b. understandable and acceptable.
   c. acceptable only if you got along.
   d. none of the above

Answer: B. But if you really didn't get along, he—and any children from their marriage who do not live with you—should not be seated near you and your family.

9. You're sending a condolence card starting with the phrase "Words can't express my sadness at hearing of your loss..." Good or bad?

Answer: Bad. If words can't express it, don't use words. Try to include a warm memory if you can, but don't rely on clichés.

10. A favorite aunt has died, and you have to decide whether or not to bring your four-year-old daughter to her funeral. You:

    a. ask the child if she wants to go.

    b. consult a child psychologist.

    c. evaluate your daughter's emotional maturity.

    d. bring her, but be prepared to leave if she becomes disruptive.

Answer: C. You thought it was D, didn't you? That is the way to go if you decide your daughter is ready for the experience, but you have to make that determination first. If she's not ready, get a baby-sitter.

11. Your detested boss is dead, and you're approaching his wife at the funeral. Your first words:

    a. "He was a prince."

    b. "He was a swine."

    c. "Are you dating yet?"

    d. "I'm so sorry for your loss."

Answer: D. Don't be a hypocrite, but don't hurt the woman unnecessarily. If you answered C, deduct ten points from your score and start reading this book again from page 1.

12. A friend has fallen ill, and you're calling to offer support. You say:

    a. "Let me know what I can do."

    b. "Do you need food?"

    c. "Let me pick up your dry cleaning."

    d. all of the above

Answer: D. Offering help is fine, but being specific is better. If your friend—or whoever is caring for her—doesn't suggest something specific, offer something yourself.

13. The proper order of support, from best to worst, for a sick friend:

    a. visit, phone, E-mail, fax, note.

b. visit, note, phone, E-mail, fax.

c. phone, visit, fax, E-mail, note.

d. note, phone, visit, fax, E-mail.

Answer: A. A note or letter is too slow. If you can't do any of the rest, rely on it as a last resort.

14. You're visiting a sick friend who needs cheering up. You bring:

a. flowers.

b. food.

c. a video.

d. all of the above

Answer: D. And make the video a comedy or a musical.

15. You see your sick friend for the first time since his illness, and he looks awful. You tell him he looks good. Good or bad?

Answer: Bad. He knows how he looks. Concentrate on what he's doing to get well, and don't lie to your friend.

16. You've been ill, and friends have been bringing gifts and flowers. You:

a. must send thank you notes immediately.

b. should send thank you notes when you feel up to it.

c. can fax or E-mail thank yous

d. none of the above

Answer: B. Thank you notes are an obligation. You need to fulfill it, and do so when you can. If you need to write ten, but you can only write two today, write two. Nobody expects you to be a hero for thank you notes, but you can't just forget about your well-wisher's thoughts, either. Write the notes.

17. You've been fired from your job. Your first concern should be:

a. finding out why you were fired.

    b.   getting a letter of reference.
    c.   seeing if your car lease is returnable.
    d.   setting fire to your boss's desk.

Answer: A. If you know why, you can prevent it from happening again. You can't reverse the firing, and if it was for poor performance rather than because of company issues like downsizing or layoffs, you'll need to address your performance in future jobs.

18. A letter of reference is:
    a.   standard from an employer to an ex-employee.
    b.   a matter of choice on the part of the employer.
    c.   a matter of choice on the part of the employee.
    d.   unimportant.

Answer: B. Ask the employer for a letter, but if you were fired for cause or poor performance, don't expect one. And read it before you use it.

19. Your sadistic boss has fired you, and you want to give him a piece of your mind. You:
    a.   write a letter to your boss, then burn it.
    b.   write a letter to your boss, then mail it.
    c.   call your boss and yell at him.
    d.   none of the above

Answer: A. Vent your feelings, then destroy the evidence before it can do you any harm.

20. Your friend and coworker has been fired. You:
    a.   stay away from him to avoid rubbing it in.
    b.   quit in solidarity.
    c.   invite him out to dinner.
    d.   none of the above

Answer: C. Offer emotional support and emphasize that you're still friends. Don't be surprised if he's angry.

21. You're an employer and an employee of yours is perform-
ing below your standards. You:
   a. fire him, but give him a letter of recommendation.
   b. fire him and withhold the letter.
   c. give him a warning and see if his performance
       improves.
   d. none of the above

Answer: C. Maybe this firing can be avoided. Try to help him
by being very specific about his performance problems, and set
a date to evaluate his progress. If there is no progress, you will
have to fire him.

22. When firing an employee, it's best to have in the room:
   a. witnesses.
   b. security personnel.
   c. a list of the employee's benefits and severance
       package.
   d. all of the above

Answer: D. Of course, A and B are necessary only if you feel
the employee might become emotional or violent, or might be
litigious later on.

Score

    0–19: You're not reading very carefully.
  20–39: Doing better, but you might want to review the
           section.
  40–59: You're getting about half of it.
  60–89: You knew some of this going in, didn't you?
90–110: You're an expert on grief. Is this a good thing?

8

High-Tech Etiquette

BETTER ISN'T ALWAYS BETTER

These are the days of miracle and wonder.
—Paul Simon, from the lyrics to "The Boy in the Bubble"

Maybe so, but they're also the days of convenience over thoughtfulness and printed-out E-mails taking the place of handwritten notes. Progress isn't always a good thing.

Let me be clear, here: technology is a grand thing. Computers, voice mail, fax machines, E-mail, call waiting, the Internet, the Web, interactive television—these are all wonderful things. Mostly, they are wonderful things in business settings, but social situations, awkward or otherwise, are another story. It's one thing to receive a sales order by fax. It's quite another to receive a wedding invitation that way.

If you've read into this book this far, you must believe that there is a value to etiquette and considerate behavior. So, to contrast that sort of behavior—doing what you wish others would do for you—with the crass, expedient practice of sending social correspondence through E-mail, or faxing when one could pick up a pen and write, is like comparing a long-stem rose with a laser-printed picture of one. It's the same flower, but the picture doesn't smell nearly as sweet.

I said earlier that technology is the enemy of reverence. It is also the enemy of consideration, and that is no small thing. Consideration, after all, is the art of doing for someone else what you believe they would like for you to do, of anticipating their hopes and fulfilling them, possibly before the other person knows what those hopes are.

With technology, ease is all. That is, high-tech devices are invented and designed with the explicit purpose of helping people do things easier. But sometimes the very effort you put into something *is* the point; the gesture is the message. If you send someone a handwritten note for no particular reason, no matter what words you happen to write, the message will be: I was thinking of you. If you E-mail that same note to the same person, the message you're conveying is: I was thinking of you, and it was easier to just tap out the note and hit "Send."

Aesthetics, after all, do stand for something, or everything we put into our homes or put onto ourselves would be the same color. It does make a difference that a note is on paper, that it is written in your own handwriting, that it conveys thoughts sent directly from your hand to the recipient's. Let's take a slightly different look at the Tiffany Theory: If you send a handwritten note on notepaper, you are sending a Tiffany note. Something you type on a computer screen and send across the Internet is the same message purchased at Woolworth's.

Faxing is even less personal than E-mail, in a way. Fax machines tend to be in high-traffic areas in offices, even in homes. And so, when you send a message via fax, you don't know for sure that the person for whom the note is intended is the one who will see it first. For that matter, you don't know if the person for whom the note is intended will see it at all.

The Pecking Order for Notes

1. A handwritten note
2. A handwritten note

3. A handwritten note
4. E-mail
5. Fax

Sundays are good days to relax, to kick back, and to do some thinking, an activity we don't always have time for during the work week. Think about the week that has just ended. Which people were especially important to you this week? Who have you been missing lately? Who needs a little emotional pick-me-up?

Now, get out your notepaper. Sit down with a cup of any liquid you happen to find relaxing, pick up a pen, and write to each one of the people whose names just suggested themselves to you.

Write that you were thinking of her. Write that you miss him. Write that you appreciate what she did for you this week, and you just want her to know. Above all, write. It is a dying art, and one that must be preserved.

Writing can be anything from a form of communication to a form of self-evaluation. One of America's most successful writers, Neil Simon, once said that "writing is self-analysis." If you have hit the wall with a problem, emotional or practical, business or personal, sit down and write. Write anything that comes into your head. Write until you feel better, or you get writer's cramp—but write.

When you're writing to the people who are special to you, it is important that you do so in your own handwriting. It is the sign that the message comes from you, and couldn't have been sent by anyone else. After all, typed words may come from anybody.

In these fast-paced days it's tempting to give in to the technological revolution. After all, technology has brought us a lot of real benefits. It improves our access to information we might not have had otherwise; it expands our possibilities for entertainment a thousandfold; and in some cases it improves our health. Technology can do many amazing things.

The important thing to remember about technology is that it was created by people to be used by people, and that is the message the designers of our most high-tech gadgets are sending us: we did this for you, to make your lives easier and more enjoyable. It is a fine message, but we have to remember that they expressed it personally. It is our job to do the same.

Nobody wants handwriting to die. Nobody thinks it's a good thing that people don't write letters anymore. There are some great benefits to technology, but there are drawbacks as well. We have to keep ourselves aware of our past and our present before we can face our future, and handwritten notes are one tiny example of how we hold on to our heritage.

If you disagree, send me a note. But please, don't E-mail or fax it.

NETIQUETTE

"The difference between reality and unreality is that reality has so little to recommend it."

—ALLAN SHERMAN, *A Gift of Laughter*

You can't deny technology. It is here, and going to be used, whether we like it or not. So while it is clearly preferable to use our own handwriting to communicate, pick up a phone, or better yet, be in the same room with another person, we have to face the reality of the twenty-first century, that computer communication is here to stay. But nobody says we have to like it.

Since that is the given, let's discuss the idea of etiquette on the Internet, because much of the communication being done these days moves across fiber-optic cables from computer to computer. An entirely new branch of etiquette, in fact, which has been given the rather obvious nickname netiquette, has sprung up, and the rules it espouses are very specific, and often unknown to online newcomers.

What, then, must you know to use your Social I.Q. on the Internet?

Most real-time communication on the Internet (that is, the closest thing to face-to-face) is done in chat rooms, where computer users gather to discuss a topic, usually something of interest to all the users who seek out that room. Rooms are devoted to virtually every possible interest on earth, from archery to the zodiac.

The new user "entering" a chat room will not know that the use of capital letters, for example, is considered rude. (By "entering," we mean going to that particular area of the Internet; there's no actual traveling involved.) Hitting the CAPS LOCK key and WRITING IN ALL CAPITALS is called shouting on the Net, and will be quickly pointed out, often in somewhat rude terms. Best to avoid it.

Also, people who send their messages in

v
e
r
t
i
c
a
l

l
i
n
e
s

are considered very rude, and will often be shunned entirely by the group. This is a form of disruption, as would be entering a movie fan chat room and discussing motorcycles.

In fact, there's an entirely new form of rudeness on the Net called spamming. Unwanted junk E-mail, usually promoting some sort of get-rich-quick scheme or chain letters, sent without the recipient's permission, is called spam. Clearly, this is the worst in Net taste, and is considered absolutely unthinkable in online circles.

It's seductive to sit for hours in a chat room, using a screen name that gives no indication of your true identity, and send out messages without thinking ahead of time that there are, in fact, other people reading them. Sending a thoughtless message can lead to "flaming," which is a kind of cyber-posse atmosphere in which other computer users criticize your message to the point of distraction. Flaming aside, it is very rude to criticize other people's opinions or their ability to communicate those opinions. And it is just as rude to flame those with whom you disagree. The bottom line: think before you hit "Send."

Bulletin board services are another area in which computer users communicate. This is less immediate, since messages are posted, then responded to, and then answered, only as people log on to a certain area and read over the messages. It's not a chat in cyber-terms, since the people communicating are not all present online at once, and the messages are not read and responded to immediately.

Flaming and spamming are just as prevalent in bulletin board services as in chat rooms, but it's easier to avoid them, since the posts on bulletin boards have more time to be considered. It's very simple: Just don't say anything to anyone else that you wouldn't want said to you.

No discussion of online communication is complete without a note of warning: you don't know who the other people on the Internet actually are. It's easy for people to take on screen names and entire personalities that aren't really theirs. Don't agree to meet with anyone you've started communicating with online unless it's in a public place and you're bringing someone you can trust. Don't assume that anybody is who they say they are. Use extreme caution and be polite, but not overly familiar. Be careful. Don't give anyone your phone number or home address. Social I.Q. demands that you be polite, but also that you remain safe.

WRITING IS BETTER THAN TALKING

I can't understand why a person would take a year to write a novel when he can easily buy one for a few dollars.

—FRED ALLEN

The most revolutionary, but perhaps the simplest, piece of technology we have in our homes is the telephone. Nothing has changed our lives quite so much, and is so taken for granted in our lives. We don't even consider the phone a technological device anymore. After all, you don't have to plug it in (well, some you don't).

But the real test of a technological leap is the impact it has on our lives, and the telephone is unparalleled in that category. Before its inception, our lives were very different, and it is impossible to go back. Now telephones are everywhere: our homes, our offices, our cars, our pockets. We can find anyone anywhere at any time with telephones, and they're easy—that's the important part—telephones are seductively easy. Just pick one up on impulse and you're communicating, literally in seconds.

That is where the danger lies. Telephones are so easy that we don't think before we pick one up—they're the communications equivalent of an impulse purchase.

Writing, on the other hand, is something that requires planning. It requires thought; it seems awfully old-fashioned and difficult; and it makes our wrists hurt just to think about it. Why write, when you can pick up a phone and call?

Because it's better, that's why.

Writing is better *because* you have to think about it. It's better *because* it requires planning and forethought. It's better because it requires you to be more precise about your message, and it gives you the opportunity to cross out what you didn't mean and start again.

Now, what should you be writing?

Letters. Cards. Thank you notes. Messages. Your true feelings. Communication.

You don't have to sit down and write a novel. You don't have to be producing a great work of drama or an exposé of a corrupt industry. Nobody is telling you to become a famous novelist or journalist. I'm telling you to write, whatever you want to write.

Write to your friends, your relatives, especially those who live in a different city. Call when you have something to say that can't wait, but write when you want to convey information in your own way, and make it special. People still love receiving letters. Think of how you feel on those rare occasions when the mail contains something other than bills and advertisements. But if you don't have enough to say to fill a letter, or the idea of writing one intimidates you, notes are just fine.

You've read about the importance of sending thank you notes, and they are very important as an acknowledgment of someone else's thoughtfulness and an expression of your own. They are an absolute necessity for anyone with manners, and something that, in this age of fax and E-mail, is in danger of going the way of the pterodactyl.

But beyond thank you notes, notes from one friend to another, simply expressing a sentiment—gratitude, concern, joy, warmth—are little blessings in an envelope. They are all too rarely written and sent, and because of our current preoccupation with other, less personal forms of communication, they are cherished when received. Write a note. Strengthen a friendship.

Beyond that, write because it *feels* good. Getting your exact feeling on paper is a sensation unequaled in today's society. It's the most satisfying feeling on earth. Try it, you'll see.

If you try it and still think I'm wrong, write me a letter and tell me so. I'll be glad to hear from you.

COMMUNICATION IS MORE IMPORTANT

When you have nothing to say, say nothing.
— CHARLES CALEB COLTON

These days, when we think of communication, we think of it as an industry, an activity, an infrastructure—anything except an art.

The truth is, though, that in these days of instant communication, big-business communication and high-tech communication, the whole idea of communication is much more important than it has ever been before, and those who can successfully practice the art of communication are at a distinct advantage over those who cannot.

Consider that Ronald Reagan, arguably one of the most successful presidents of the postmodern era, was known as the Great Communicator not because of his ideas, but because of his skill in explaining them to the public in terms that were easily understood and generally persuasive. No matter what you think of his policies, it can't be questioned that Reagan was an expert at rallying public support for them, and he did it through the art of communication.

One of Reagan's speechwriters, Peggy Noonan, writes in her book *Simply Speaking* that "Postmodern America is becoming what it was a hundred years ago: a big Chattaqua Circuit where everyone goes to listen or talk... But now, the audience is bigger, the event is being broadcast, and a certain ease is expected."

In other words, technology and communication are blending, and those who are uninterested or unskilled in communication are, plain and simple, going to be left behind.

Communication is not just writing, although that is a major part of the process. It is also the art of talking to one person or hundreds of people in roughly the same manner—to explain what you mean in ways that are easy to understand and persuasive at the same time—and the best communicators are those who can do all that without having their audiences notice that it's being done.

How can you do that? What does it have to do with Social I.Q.?

Anyone can communicate. Few people are as successful in communication as the brilliant physicist Dr. Stephen Hawking, and he is physically incapable of speech. Dr. Hawking has used technology to simulate speech because his ideas could not be held back by something as beside-the-point as his own physical disability. His intellect wouldn't allow it. And through a computer-generated voice, Dr. Hawking is as eloquent and persuasive as Ronald Reagan. It's not just the actor's natural gifts, then, that make a great communicator.

Communicating successfully is simply a question of determining your message (what point you want to get across), identifying the best way to convey that message (through humor, earnestness, anecdotes, etc.), and delivering that message in a relaxed, conversational tone, no matter how large or small your audience may be.

It sounds simple; in theory, it is simple. In practice, though, it can sometimes be a little more complicated, and that's where Social I.Q. comes in.

First of all, having good manners is in itself a form of communication. By acting in the ways set down in this book, you are communicating to the people you know (and even the ones you don't) that certain styles of behavior are important to you, and by extension, you believe they should be important to them. You are communicating by example.

But the nuts-and-bolts of communication are present in Social I.Q., too. All those thank you notes you've been writing have honed your writing skills. All that teaching, healing, and ministering you've been doing have improved your conversational skills and made you a more adept persuader. The Tiffany Theory has helped you understand how to create a message—even an unpleasant one—and make it palatable to your audience. You've practiced your communication skills on your family, your spouse, your romantic partners. You've gotten into other people's hats, and tried to understand what makes them think the way they do. Once you can empathize like that, you are well on your way to being a great communicator.

Technology? It's a tool, or a series of tools. I'm writing this book on a computer because writing it in longhand would take far too much time and be much less efficient. I use faxes and E-mail. I leave messages for people on their voice mail, and hope they'll leave me messages on mine. I'm not antitechnology. I'm for using technology to communicate better, because communication is more important now than ever before, and will become even more important into the next millennium.

WHEN TECHNOLOGY IS BETTER

I don't necessarily agree with everything I say.
—MARSHALL McLUHAN

You've read the last few chapters and concluded that technology is the enemy of reverence, and the enemy of consideration. You might have concluded that I am an enemy of technology. Not at all.

Technology can be a wonderful thing when it's used to communicate honest ideas and increase manners and everyone's Social I.Q. Sometimes technology—fax machines, E-mail, the Internet, even telephones—can be the perfect thing to make your communication more efficient and more successful, and anything that does that can't be all bad.

The trick, then, is to know when to use technology, and how. In what situations is technology the way to go?

When speed is the most important concern. If you have information that must be communicated immediately, obviously writing letters and going to speak face-to-face with people is going to be too slow. Use the phone, the fax, the modem.

When your audience is much too large for you to communicate with each one directly. If you're trying to generate publicity, for example, to help your business, then you have to reach a lot of people quickly—through television, newspapers, radio, the Internet.

When geography plays a role in your message. If your audience, even of one person, is so far away that a visit is an impossibility, and you need to communicate your idea in less than the three to five days it might take to send a note by mail, the telephone is the way to go. A voice-to-voice conversation is certainly better than E-mail, though, and we've discussed the problems with faxes and their inherent lack of privacy.

When technology is part of your message. If, for example, your audience is likely to be found only on a computer bulletin board, it is clear that calling or writing to each of these people would be impractical and unnecessary. Don't fight technology simply because it's technology; use it when it makes sense to use it.

Remember that all the technological miracles and wonders devised in the twentieth century are tools, and they're meant to be used. It is in the *way* you choose to use them, through the clever and creative things you do with them, that you create an art: the art of communication. And communicating with other people, coupled with a strong Social I.Q., is an art that can make your life and the lives around you better. *That's* the ultimate goal.

THE HIGH-TECH ETIQUETTE QUIZ

Answer each question honestly. Five points for each correct answer. No peeking.

1. You have a sudden impulse to tell your mother that you think she did a fine job raising you. The best method for conveying this message is:
   a. a phone call.
   b. a handwritten note
   c. E-mail.
   d. fax.

Answer: B. Even with a sudden impulse, a handwritten note is better. The message doesn't have to be sudden, even if the thought to convey it was.

2. You had a fine time on a date last night and you'd like to tell your date that, but you only have his business card. Best medium:
   a. a handwritten note.
   b. a fax to his office.
   c. a call to his office.
   d. any of the above

Answer: A. That handwritten note is still going to be best. Even if you only have a business address, a note is going to get there in a day or two, which is plenty of time for a situation like this. A fax could be seen by anyone in his office; calling him in his office is second-best, but not even close. Five points for the handwritten note.

3. You've just entered an online chat room, and suddenly you're besieged with messages urging you to stop shouting. You are:
   a. sending messages about a topic other than the one discussed in this room.
   b. monopolizing the conversation.
   c. using all capital letters.
   d. sending messages vertically rather than horizontally.

Answer: C. The use of all capital letters is considered rude online, and does stand out rather obviously. Get off that CAPS LOCK key.

4. You've been online two weeks and suddenly you're being spammed. This means:
   a. people are making rude remarks about you.
   b. you're receiving canned meat in the mail.
   c. you're being asked to leave a chat room.
   d. you're receiving unwanted E-mail soliciting money.

Answer: D. This is considered extremely rude and is unquestionably annoying. The only recourse is to contact your online provider for help.

5. You've left a series of posts on your computer bulletin board service (BBS), and now you're being flamed. This means:
   a. the same as being spammed.
   b. receiving extreme criticism of your post.
   c. being asked to leave the BBS.
   d. none of the above

Answer: B. Large quantities of criticism of your posts is called flaming, and is very inconsiderate. Your only recourse is to avoid escalating the argument and to think more carefully when posting in the future. Take the high road.

6. You've just received a lovely gift in the mail from your cousin, who lives two thousand miles away (don't worry, this isn't a math question). You should:
   a. call her immediately to thank her and let her know the gift has arrived undamaged.
   b. send a thank you note, handwritten.
   c. both A and B
   d. none of the above

Answer: C. Yes, it's best to let your cousin know that the gift has arrived in good shape. That means immediacy is important, so that's a phone call situation. But it doesn't by any means relieve you of your responsibility to send a handwritten thank you note. Nice try. Two points for b.

7. Communication is best served by:
   a. the Tiffany Theory.
   b. the Ambassador Theory.
   c. a fax machine.
   d. all of the above

Answer: A. The Ambassador Theory applies in communications, as do all rules of manners. But the Tiffany Theory is a communications *tool,* meaning that it will help you communicate your message better. Think about it in conversation, business communications, and personal relationships. The more you use it, the better you'll get.

8. Your mother has passed away, and you need to contact your relatives. The best way is:
   a. a handwritten note.
   b. a death notice in the newspaper.
   c. a phone call.
   d. E-mail.

Answer: C. This is a time for speed, not aesthetics. When you have to communicate a message in a hurry, the phone is the way to go. E-mail would be tacky beyond belief; *deduct* two points if you chose d.

9. You're introducing a new product line aimed specifically at senior citizens living in warm climates. Your best medium is:
   a. television.
   b. E-mail.
   c. phone calls.
   d. a handwritten note.

Answer: A. When you're dealing with a message that has to go to a large audience, technology isn't just acceptable, it's necessary. Television is the fastest way, but it's expensive to advertise. Brochures, newspaper and magazine ads, and radio are alternatives for a budget, but mass media is definitely the way to go here.

10. You want to reach an audience of comic book enthusiasts to ask them a question about a specific superhero for a book you're writing. Your best method is:
    a. a handwritten note.
    b. a computer bulletin board.
    c. television.
    d. newspaper ads.

Answer: B. Fastest and cheapest. Find a specific bulletin board for superhero enthusiasts, and you'll get your answer in the quickest, least expensive way you can find. Technology can, in fact, be grand.

Score

0–10: You're still washing your clothes on a rock in the stream, aren't you?

11–20: Okay, so you know how to use a telephone.

21–30: Welcome to the twentieth century.

31–40: Welcome to the twenty-first century.

41–50: You're a whiz. You get the Quill Pen and Fax Machine award for blending handwritten notes with technology.

9

Etiquette

PARTIES

Manners are a sensitive awareness of the feelings of others. If you have that awareness, you have good manners, no matter what fork you use.

—Emily Post

Traditionally, manners books have devoted themselves to social gatherings. Parties, weddings, christenings, graduations, anniversaries—these are all milestones in our lives, and we seem to be terrified that we might set a foot wrong marking one of them.

There *are* rules for behavior at parties, and some of them are worth noting. But the most important thing to remember about parties is that they are supposed to be designed for a good time, not only for the guests, but for the people who host them, too. If you make sure that every place setting is perfect, your china pattern is exquisite, your service is excellent, your wine list is impressive, and then you have a terrible time because you're so nervous that you can't enjoy yourself, the party has been a failure.

Here are a few areas in which the rules are important.

Invitations

What are you waiting for, a formal invitation? Well, if you're attending a wedding or formal dinner party, you should expect just that—an engraved, written invitation. For a formal dinner party, invitations are generally sent out three weeks before the event. For a wedding, see page 250.

With more casual parties, however, the custom these days is usually to invite by telephone. Personally, I prefer written invitations when possible, particularly for "event" parties like birthdays, graduations, or anniversaries. In the case of surprise parties, written invitations are a must, to invite the guests and to inform them that they should be keeping mum when talking to the guest of honor.

When sending written invitations, use personal stationery for more casual parties. For very casual affairs, store-bought, fill-in-the-blank invitations are acceptable.

Guest Lists

For large affairs, guest lists are actually easier to compile than for smaller gatherings. Smaller parties require a more deft touch, since it will be more obvious if guests are incompatible. Think about a seating chart even if you're not planning on having a sit-down dinner, just so you can decide who would be happiest talking with whom. If you start noticing conflicts, you may have to revise your guest list.

Write the list out on paper, and check off each name as you write (or call) the guests. You'll also be making a second check next to each name as RSVP calls start coming in.

RSVP

There is no excuse (and I mean none) for not responding to an invitation, other than not having received it. Formal invitations include response cards, which you must mail back promptly, whether you will attend or not. More casual parties will include an RSVP notice on the invitation. Some people are now actually including notations like "unless we hear otherwise, we'll be expecting you at eight." This is tricky, since some people who aren't attending will still fail to respond, and you'll have miscalculated your number of guests. It's best to stick with RSVP, and specify a date by which you expect to hear.

Telephone invitations, assuming that you speak to the person and not their voice mail, will usually receive responses immediately. Sometimes the guest will say he's not sure of his calendar and will call you back. If it's a week before the party and you still haven't heard, you should call again.

Formal Dinners

Naturally, there are more rules for formal dinners than for casual pizza get-togethers in the kitchen. While place settings, table layout, and other such details are well documented in other etiquette books, there are a few situations in which your Social I.Q. will come in handy:

Formal dinners are often served by hired help. Guests are served from the left and plates are cleared from the right. Women are generally served before men.

The host or hostess is served last.

Guests should be seated with compatibility in mind—if two people are known not to get along and both are attending, seat them as far apart as possible.

Check ahead to make sure that there are no dietary conflicts (food allergies, religious restrictions, etc.) among your guests. Vegetarians, for example, should be accommodated.

Dinner parties are about conversation and dining. As long as those two aspects are entertaining, all should go smoothly. Pay attention to detail if you're hosting, but don't lose sight of your goal—to provide and to have a good time.

WEDDINGS

Marriage is our last, best chance to grow up.
> —JOSEPH BARTH, American novelist

There is, perhaps, no ceremony in which there are more rules of etiquette than a wedding. Every aspect of this one event is placed under intense scrutiny, and every moment seems to have its own set of rules. Consequently, there are the largest number of potentially awkward situations attached to a wedding than to any other single day in one's life.

A wedding is a ritual and a celebration, often tied to a religious ceremony. The ritual and the ceremony take the lesser amount of time, and the celebration the larger, but in each half there are equal concerns about manners and etiquette.

Let's examine the planning of a wedding (which can often lay the groundwork for a divorce), and the wedding itself, in steps:

Step 1: Engagement After a couple becomes engaged, announcements are often sent to family and friends, and a printed announcement is placed in at least one local newspaper. Usually, the announcement is made by the bride's parents, but that has become flexible. Sometimes announcements are now made by both sets of parents or by the couple themselves. In today's society, it is noted in the announcement if the bride will retain her maiden name, and a date for the wedding is not included in the engagement announcement.

Step 2: Invitations Wedding invitations can be formal or informal. Formal invitations are more common, usually engraved or printed professionally (no laser printers allowed!), and include a response card to make RSVP lists easier to manage. They are traditionally sent out much earlier than those for a dinner party (six to eight weeks is not at all unusual, and some couples send them earlier), but there is no specified period of time at which the invitations must be sent. Clearly, enough time must be allowed for RSVP responses to be made and noted before a final guest count must be given to the caterer, if there is one.

Invitations are usually made by the bride's parents, or whomever is paying for the wedding. They should include the names of both the bride and groom; the date, time, and place of the wedding; and the reception invitation (which can be separate or included with the invitation to the ceremony; some couples list both on one card). A combined invitation should include an RSVP notice, including a date by which the response should be made.

Formal invitations include a separate RSVP card, with an envelope to return it (which should be stamped by the person sending the invitation).

In some cases, wedding announcements are sent. These cards announce the wedding to friends and relatives who are not being invited to the wedding, and they are sent either on the day of the wedding or shortly afterward.

Step 3: Bridal Showers and Bachelor Parties What used to be simple has become complicated by the politically correct atmosphere of the late twentieth century. Wedding showers, once reserved specifically for the bride, can now include the groom, and bachelor parties (or dinners) are now quite often thrown for both the bride and the groom, separately or (in rare instances) together.

Showers can be given at any time before the wedding, and should not be given by members of the immediate family of the person receiving the shower (or either family, in case of couple showers).

There is no rule covering the type of shower thrown. If it's not a surprise affair, the couple can help plan the event and decide what kind of shower (that is, what type of gifts) would be most appropriate. Wedding registers at stores from Neiman Marcus to Home Depot can accommodate virtually any couple.

Bachelor parties are clearly no-holds-barred affairs, but embarrassing either the bride or groom with something that won't suit their taste is inappropriate. If either wishes to have a raucous, steamy party, there's no reason not to, but if it would compromise either's dignity, it's best to try something else. A friend of mine had his bachelor party at Yankee Stadium. No strippers showed up, and no one missed them.

Step 4: The Ceremony　There are, as you well know, literally hundreds of rules covering the wedding ceremony. But this is the most important one: whatever the bride and groom feel is important must be enforced, and what is not is entirely optional.

Formal weddings, for those who desire and can afford them, are often held in churches, temples, and mosques. For those who are not religious, they can be held at catering halls, in private homes, restaurants, outdoors, or anywhere else the couple desires. Processionals generally begin the ceremony, with ushers coming down the aisle first, then bridesmaids, the maid or matron of honor, the flower girl, the ring bearer, and finally the bride, accompanied by her father if he's living and present. The groom and best man wait at the front of the room, with the clergy or official.

Obviously, the religious ceremony differs depending on the denomination involved. After the ceremony is over there is a recessional, led by the bride and groom, then the flower girl, the best man and the maid or matron of honor, the ushers, and finally the bridesmaids, usually paired by height.

Step 5: The Reception　Photographers often insist on taking photographs immediately after the receiving line has passed, so allow some time between the receiving line and the reception or there will be conflict.

According to tradition, included in the receiving line are the bride and groom's mothers, the newlywed couple, the maid of honor, and sometimes the couple's fathers. Also, sometimes included in modern receiving lines are the best man, the bridesmaids, and ushers.

After formal photographs are taken, the reception begins, often in a restaurant or reception hall separate from the site of the ceremony. Directions should be provided in the invitation.

There are many traditional elements to the reception, and brides and grooms can pick and choose as they please. A toast is virtually standard, usually given by the best man, but nowadays often it is followed by one from the maid or matron of honor and possibly other wedding party members.

The wedding cake is cut just before dessert (assuming there is a dinner), by the bride, sometimes with help from her husband. The traditional feeding of cake from the bride to groom is optional, as is the throwing of the bouquet, the garter ceremony, and the throwing of rice as the couple leaves for their honeymoon.

Step 6: Gifts It's traditional that gifts be sent within a year of the wedding. Again, wedding registers offer wide ranges of gifts, in many price ranges. Find out where the couple has registered, ask the store for a list of available gifts, and choose what fits your budget. Gifts can be sent to the address on the invitation, or on an at-home card (a card which lists where the newlywed couple will be living), if it is provided. Money is not an inappropriate gift for most couples starting a new life.

Step 7: Thank You Notes These notes absolutely must be handwritten, with a specific mention of the gift, so the bride and groom should keep a list, and keep it accurate. They should be sent promptly within four weeks of the end of the honeymoon.

Who Pays for What?

The following is a list of financial obligations that are traditionally handled by certain members of the wedding party or families involved. However, rules have changed, and nothing is set in stone. Consider this a guideline.

- Bride's Family: invitations, announcements, flowers, music, bride's gifts for bridesmaids and groom, groom's wedding ring, church fee, all reception costs.
- Groom's Family: bride's rings (both engagement and wed-

ding), presents for the bride, ushers, and best man; flowers
for the groom and ushers; clergy fee, flowers for immediate
members of both families, rehearsal dinner, bachelor party,
hotel for out-of-town ushers, honeymoon.
- Bridesmaids: dress, gift.
- Ushers: transportation to wedding, rental of tuxedo, gift,
  bachelor dinner (optional).

But, hey, remember: it's all supposed to be fun—and
meaningful.

GIFTS

Good taste is the worst vice ever invented.

—EDITH STILLWELL

You've probably noticed throughout this book that I've discussed giving gifts on a number of occasions. I did not do this
because of a childlike fascination with gifts, but as a reminder
that there are times when giving gifts is important, and that part
of developing your Social I.Q. is knowing when to give them.

The bottom line: any time you visit someone's home for the
first time, you must bring a gift. If it's a new home, something
useful might be indicated: in Jewish tradition, a loaf of bread
and a container of salt is the proscribed housewarming gift. In
modern times, those items would still be present, but might be
supplemented with something you know the new homeowner
might need.

Here are some other occasions when gifts are important, and
suggested gifts to go along with those occasions:

A dinner party. Anytime you visit for dinner (assuming
you're not just going to your best friend's house for pizza like
you do every Friday), you have to bring a gift. A bottle of wine
is always nice, unless the homeowner you're visiting is ada-
mantly opposed to alcohol. In that case, bring a vase or some

other home-related item, or ask if there's anything you can contribute to the dinner. Dessert, perhaps?

An "occasion" party. Most people think of this one first in terms of gift giving—a birthday, anniversary, graduations, a religious rite of passage (a christening, first communion, bar or bat mitzvah, etc.). In some cases (depending on the recipient and the occasion), money is an acceptable gift—for births, bar or bat mitzvahs, and some birthdays, for example. Other times, it's more generally accepted to bring a token of some sort. A chart with the traditional anniversary gifts follows this chapter.

After a first date. We discussed this before, remember? It doesn't have to be anything fancy or expensive, but if you did enjoy a first date, let the person know with something that says, "Let's do it again."

A family function. Yes, even if you're not getting along. You go to a house, you bring a gift—but keep your budget in mind. Remember, if the occasion is a dinner, you can always bring wine or food, if you ask the host or hostess which is preferred.

When someone is ill. Again, try to be empathetic. Think of what your sick friend or relative needs, and try to bring that.

When visiting someone with children. You don't always have to bring a gift for the parents, but the kids will be thrilled, and the parents will be happier than if you brought something for them.

The key to successful gift-giving is to get out of the mind-set that says, "I'll get him or her what I think she or he needs," and into one that says, "What do I think will make him or her happy?" After all, the idea of giving a gift is not to satisfy yourself that you've done something the way you wanted it to be done, but that you have contributed to someone else's life materially, and in a way that this person would want you to contribute.

In other words, it's more important to get what *they* want, not what you think they *should* want. It's a subtle distinction, but one that's very important in giving gifts.

And remember, too: It is not necessary to go into debt to buy someone else a gift, no matter how deeply you feel for that person. If they love you as well, they certainly don't want you to be paying for something for a long time to come. The thought is truly what counts, and a thinker with a strong Social I.Q. can come up with something that will be appropriate, bring true happiness to its recipient, and not break the gift-giver's budget. Happy hunting.

Anniversary Gifts

First: paper, plastic, or clocks
Second: cotton
Third: leather or glass
Fourth: linen
Fifth: wood
Sixth: iron
Seventh: copper or wool
Eighth: bronze or electrical appliances
Ninth: pottery
Tenth: tin or aluminum
Eleventh: steel
Twelfth: silk or linen
Thirteenth: lace
Fourteenth: ivory
Fifteenth: crystal or glass
Twentieth: china or platinum jewelry
Twenty-fifth: silver
Thirtieth: pearl
Thirty-fifth: jade or coral
Fortieth: ruby or garnet
Forty-fifth: sapphire
Fiftieth: gold
Sixtieth: diamond
After that, you're on your own.

Birthstones

January: garnet
February: amethyst
March: aquamarine

April: diamond
May: emerald
June: pearl
July: ruby
August: peridot
September: sapphire
October: opal
November: topaz
December: turquoise

LIVING IN SOCIETY

*Here's my Golden Rule for a tarnished age: Be fair with
others, and then keep after them until they're fair with
you.*

—ALAN ALDA

Social I.Q. isn't an isolated concept; that is, you can't practice it
in a vacuum. No man is an island, and all that. We are members
of society (from which the word "social" comes, after all), and
we have to interact with the other members. If we didn't, we
wouldn't need a Social I.Q. at all; we'd just all do whatever we
wanted all the time.

There are basic rules to living in society; most of them are
called laws, and there's no need for us to examine those here.
They're well documented, and the consequences of breaking
them are clear.

Social laws, however, are somewhat more hazy, and to break
one, quite often, is a question of not doing something right
rather than doing something wrong.

Silence Is Agreement

There is a Jewish proverb that says, "Silence is agreement."
This means that if you see a social wrong—not an etiquette

problem, necessarily, but something that should not be tolerated in society—and you don't protest its practice, you are tacitly giving your approval to that wrong. For example, a friend of yours tells you a joke that is offensive in its portrayal of homosexuals. You can react in two ways: you can pretend to find the joke funny, or you can tell your friend that it's offensive, and why.

This situation is similar to one we discussed earlier, but it's important to see the distinction here, which can come down to another simple adage: if you're not part of the solution, you're part of the problem.

Remember the ripple effect? How the good feelings you generate through Social I.Q. can grow through the people whose lives you touch? Well, the same thing is true of negative energy. Do nothing, and your friend thinks that his joke was appropriate and acceptable. The consequence is clear: he'll tell it again...and again. Maybe some of the people he tells it to will retell it. The negative stereotype will continue to spread, and not only will no good be done, but the situation will actually be worse than when it started, with your friend telling you a joke.

You know how to deal with this. Your reaction is exactly the same as in the other situation, when racial remarks were made in the locker room. And it's just as imperative that you take that step and make the move, because a negative stereotype against any group will weaken our society. Use the Tiffany Theory, but make sure that you go ahead and say something. Break the chain as quickly as you can, before it goes past you and becomes stronger.

Touchy Subjects

There are some things you don't want to talk about. I don't mean secrets; I mean subjects that you're not comfortable discussing. Everybody has some, but not everyone's are the same. You may stumble onto a problem area without even knowing it's a problem.

The brilliant comedy writer Larry Gelbart, who developed

and produced $M\star A\star S\star H$ for television, once noted that when he was writing that show, he found the network censors' most touchy area.

"Religion," he said, "is more sensitive than sex; it's more sensitive than politics; it's more sensitive than violence." In his portrayal of the fictional army unit's chaplain, a Roman Catholic priest, Gelbart found that he had stumbled over the most difficult area for his network to handle, and had to be very careful about what he had the priest do and say.

It's the same with our daily relationships. Religion is a very difficult subject for many people to discuss; they're sometimes dogmatic, sometimes angry, sometimes downright embarrassed or afraid. But unless someone actually brings up the subject with you, you could do worse than assume religion is something another person doesn't want to discuss.

On the other hand, everyone seems to want to discuss politics. The problem is, very few people can agree when the subject arises. There has rarely been a political discussion held in this country. What we have are political arguments, even among members of the same party and with the same philosophy. Everyone sees everything his own way.

It's hard to avoid talking about politics. What you have to do is send out a few feelers before expressing a strong opinion, especially when talking with people who might have an impact on your business or your personal relationships. If they disagree strongly, you're likely to have a problem on your hands.

Instead of stating your own political view at the beginning of a conversation and waiting for the other person to agree or disagree, simply bring up the topic— "I see the president's getting ready to sign that anti–fox-hunting law"—and see what reaction you get. Your position (that is, your conversational position, not your political view, which is your own and your right) will depend on how the other person responds.

If, for example, the person you're talking to snorts and says, "Yeah, now we're going to be overrun with foxes; I don't know how that guy got elected," you have a clear view of his political view. If you happen to be in favor of a fox-hunting ban, you can choose to argue the point with this man, or, if you decide you don't want to risk it, you can change the subject.

If you decide to argue the point, be prepared to face the consequences. People take their political point of view very seriously, and often resent anyone expressing an opposing view. If you're willing to take that risk, go ahead and play fox's advocate. If not, start discussing your favorite sports team. But true fans are usually pretty touchy about that sort of thing, too, so...

How to Get Out of an Argument

Notice that the heading is not "How to Win an Argument." There are hundreds of books on that subject, and any one of them will either help you win arguments or send you off in search of another book. What we're discussing here is how to *end* an argument.

You can concede.   If your adversary has made her point too compelling for you to continue, you can merely say, "You know, maybe you're right," and let it go at that. Few people have that clear-eyed a view in the heat of battle, however, so don't expect it to happen too often.

You can agree to disagree.   This is increasingly popular among people who don't have a lot of time to waste. At some point, you can merely acknowledge that you have opposing views and that you are very unlikely to change them no matter how strong the arguments in either direction. You can simply agree to change the subject at that point, and move on. The upside is that the argument is over; the downside, that either you or the other person may harbor negative feelings from it.

You can provide proof.   In those cases when the argument is simple enough to make, you can provide a book, expert, or reference source that will decide the question. This works only when a fact, and not an opinion, is being argued. If the question is: "Did Cameron Mitchell or Jack Palance play that role?" the facts can be substantiated in a book or on a web site, and one arguer or another will clearly win. If it's: "Was Cameron

Mitchell a better actor than Jack Palance?" there is no clear answer, and you'd best read over the first two suggestions again.

No matter what, you should enter an argument with the view that people's opinions are rarely changed without a very strong reason. If you know what you're trying to achieve when you begin, and roughly how much you can expect to achieve, and—most important—you know when to quit, you can have arguments without damaging your business or professional relationships.

HUMOR

Nothing in man is more serious than his sense of humor;
it is the sign that he wants all the truth.

—CARL VAN DOREN

A sense of humor may be the greatest gift we humans received from the force that created us; it is certainly the thing that can be counted on to keep us sane when all is dark. As Jean Kerr wrote in *Please Don't Eat the Daisies,* "if you can keep your head when all about you are losing theirs, it's just possible you haven't grasped the situation."

Never underestimate humor; it is far more important to our lives than we usually admit. It can also create some of the most awkward situations, or at least the most awkward moments, of our lives. Remember, Murphy was an optimist.

Everyone has made a remark or told a joke and had it fall flat. That uncomfortable silence may be the most difficult sound to endure on the planet. Ask any comic who's bombed in a comedy club.

Let's see how we can avoid that situation with a little foresight and a little observation: first of all, consider your audience. If they're all under twenty-five, they might not catch the reference to *I Dream of Jeannie*. Heck, they may not be old enough to remember *Seinfeld*.

Also, keep in mind that almost all humor is guaranteed to be offensive to *somebody*. But ethnic jokes, jokes that belittle people based on their religion, sexual orientation, or appearance are virtually always offensive, or should be, to *everyone*. They are exactly the kind of negative energy that pollute our environment far more completely than secondhand smoke or car exhaust. Until we can rid ourselves of our prejudices about each other, we will be unable to inhabit this planet peacefully, and until we can stop giving tacit approval to hate by laughing at jokes at some group's expense—perpetuating stereotypes and increasing mistrust and dislike—all of us will be guilty of complicity. Remember, silence is agreement.

Now, it's also true that these same jokes, when told *within the group being ridiculed*—that is, a Jew or an African American telling Jewish or African American jokes, etc.—are usually accepted. That's not right and not fair, but it's often true.

The best and safest kind of humor to use in groups is self-deprecating humor. Make fun of yourself and people will likely laugh along with you. Make fun of them, and they'll more likely be offended and hold a grudge.

The Ambassador Theory is at work here, although it may be somewhat hard to see how. Keep in mind that making a joke at your own expense is a way of avoiding making a joke at someone else's. In that way, you're taking the heat off everyone who is listening to the joke and avoiding confrontations that could lead to their thinking ill of you. You are an ambassador for that smallest subset—yourself.

HUMOR TO AVOID AT PARTIES

- Ethnic jokes (meaning all jokes at the expense of any group)
- Jokes about a health condition—someone there may have it

- "Humorous" innuendoes about couples present—their marriage is none of your business
- Jokes about sex if they contain offensive language or your audience is not open to explicit talk
- Jokes about professions—you don't know who the lawyers are

It's often been noted that when speaking to a group, you should open with a joke. Keep the rule about jokes within a group in mind—if you are a member, you can probably get away with it, since it would be seen as self-deprecating humor. If you're not, don't take a chance that you'll annoy your audience with the first words out of your mouth.

Joking on dates can be another source of trouble. On first dates, especially, a difference in taste—meaning that you think something is funny and your date doesn't—could be extremely damaging, particularly if you're truly interested in this person and want to have a second date. Be careful.

The bottom line is that some people have the knack to be funny, while some people are better at appreciating humor. There's nothing on this planet more awkward than listening to someone who is not naturally funny try to prove he is. Assess yourself carefully and honestly. If you're one of those people who is meant to be part of the audience, accept your role gladly. There's no reason to be ashamed. George Washington wasn't a laugh riot by any stretch of the imagination, and look how far he got in life.

Humor is to be appreciated. If no one is laughing, there is no joke. Be proud to be one of the laughers, and allow the comedian his role. After all, if everybody could be funny, they wouldn't pay Jim Carrey $20 million a movie.

THE ETIQUETTE QUIZ

Please be polite while answering, and award yourself five points for each correct response. If you are rude during answering, deduct two points. Tally the points up at the end, and be glad there's only one more quiz on the book after this one.

1. A party is successful if:
   a. all the rules of etiquette are followed.
   b. the guests have a good time.
   c. no rules are followed, but the host has a good time.
   d. the guests and the host have a good time.

Answer: D. The rules are meant to help you have a good time by eliminating decisions you'd otherwise have to consider. If you and your guests enjoy yourself, it's a successful party.

2. Invitations to a dinner party should be:
   a. engraved.
   b. written.
   c. telephoned.
   d. E-mailed.

Answer: B. Engraving for a simple dinner party is too much. Telephone or E-mail is too little. And store-bought, fill-in-the-blanks invitations are only acceptable for children's parties or very informal affairs.

3. It is an absolute necessity to repsond to an invitation, even if no RSVP request is written on the invitation. True or false?

Answer: True. Although the person doing the inviting *should* include a request to RSVP, and a phone number or address at which to do so, the invitation itself implies a response. Not responding at all is unbearably rude.

4. Engagement announcements should be sent by:
    a. the bride's family.
    b. the groom's family.
    c. both families.
    d. the couple themselves.
    e. any of the above

Answer: E. Things have become flexible in this area, although the strict rule still requires the bride's family to do the announcing. At this point, so long as the announcement is made properly, it doesn't matter who does it.

5. Wedding invitations should be sent:
    a. six to eight weeks before the wedding.
    b. eight to ten weeks before the wedding.
    c. four to six weeks before the wedding.
    d. up to a year before the wedding.

Answer: A. Enough time to clear the date and respond properly, but not so much time that the date is likely to be forgotten.

6. At a wedding, the most important consideration in planning the day is:
    a. the time of year.
    b. the rules of etiquette.
    c. the individual preferences of the couple.
    d. the pleasure of the guests.

Answer: Believe it or not, C. This is the one chance the couple gets to do things their way all day. The rules of etiquette are guidelines. Of course, if the couple does things in such a way as to be rude to their guests, they are not being good hosts, and should consider this before enacting the plan.

7. Wedding gifts must be sent:
   a. within four weeks of the wedding, either before or after.
   b. to arrive on the day of the wedding.
   c. within six months of the wedding.
   d. within a year of the wedding.

Answer: D. One year after the wedding is the traditional period to send a gift.

8. Thank you notes should be sent:
   a. within four weeks of the end of the honeymoon.
   b. within a week of the wedding.
   c. within six months of the wedding.
   d. within a year of the wedding.

Answer: A. Of course, if the gift arrives after that period, the couple has four weeks from the arrival of the gift to send a thank-you note.

9. Gift-giving is about:
   a. getting someone the most expensive thing you can afford.
   b. getting someone what they want.
   c. getting someone what you think they should have.
   d. making a gesture and not looking cheap.

Answer: B. What you have decided someone needs is not the point. You're trying to make a friendly gesture and do something the other person would like for you to do. This isn't about you; it's about *them*.

10. Silence is:
   a. golden.
   b. an indication of a hearing problem.
   c. agreement.
   d. all of the above

Answer: C. When you see or hear something offensive or

hurtful and you do nothing, you are part of the problem, not part of the solution. Go back and read the chapter again if you need hints on how to deal with such a situation, but do something.

Score

    0–10: Put the remote control down and read the chapter again.

11–20: Emily Post is sending enforcers to your house. Practice more.

21–30: You're an average American. Work on it.

31–40: Definite improvement, but your tuxedo has a spot.

41–50: The Fred Astaire Award.

10

And in Conclusion...

Q&A WITH THE AUTHOR: FAQS

A person who publishes a book willfully appears before the populace with his pants down.

—EDNA ST. VINCENT MILLAY

Okay, so you've read through all my advice, and hopefully you've found my arguments compelling and sensible. You know about thank you notes and sex, you've read my views on family relations, marriage, children, and humor. You're well versed in the Tiffany Theory, the Ambassador Theory, the roles of teacher, healer, and minister, and you've taken more quizzes than you can remember taking since high school—but there's one big one yet to come, so don't feel like you're through yet!

Perhaps somewhere along the line you've wondered: Why the heck should I be listening to this guy? What makes him such an expert? Who is Michael Levine, anyway?

Well, hopefully the first couple of chapters in this book gave you my basic background, but just in case you still have questions about Social I.Q., this chapter is here to help.

People often ask me questions about my theories and some of the ideas put down in this book. I'm going to save you the time and energy, and ask them myself. Then I'll also answer them myself.

What follows, then, represents the most frequently asked questions about the Social I.Q. system and how I developed it. I have avoided asking myself personal questions, since as we know from Chapter 39, they can be rude, and I wouldn't want to be rude with myself. But I have asked the questions that I think can help you understand and apply Social I.Q. best. So here goes:

Q. Nice seeing you, Michael.

A. Thank you, Michael. Let me just say you're looking wonderful.

Q. You flatter me. Tell me, how did you develop your Social I.Q.?

A. Well, it took years, let me tell you. I developed the theory of Social I.Q. through carefully observing people and reading many important books, like M. Scott Peck's *The Road Less Traveled,* William Bennett's *Book of Virtues, Getting the Love You Want,* by Harville Hendrix, and *Seven Habits of Highly Effective People,* by Stephen Covey, among many others. But I developed my own Social I.Q. the way everyone else usually does—by making most of the mistakes I talk about in the book. The difference was that I had trained myself to examine human interactions, so when I made one of these mistakes—showing up without a gift to a dinner party, for example—I was aware of what I had done, why it was a mistake, and how it made the people I dealt with feel. And I resolved not to make the same mistake twice. That's what a Social I.Q. is all about—not making the same mistake twice. You shouldn't feel like a failure if you make a mistake, but learn from those you do make.

Q. You also talk about the society in general becoming less mannered. Did that lead to your writing this book?

A. Sure. Part of the observation process I was talking about was the inevitable conclusion that our society is becoming more coarse. While most people didn't seem to see that as a problem, I did. I think that the less consideration people show for each other, the worse off our society and the world around us will be. It doesn't matter if you eat your salad with your dessert fork, but it does matter if you don't treat people the way you want them to treat you.

Q. Can you handle any awkward situation?

A. Me, personally? Of course not. No one can. But people who develop their Social I.Q., their ability to notice, analyze, and not repeat their mistakes, have a much better chance of anticipating awkward situations, and generally will be able to improvise through a sticky moment. I have managed to develop my own Social I.Q. to the point where I can usually see an awkward situation coming, but life has a way of constantly surprising us. One major step is in acknowledging that the situation *is* awkward. If you have an elephant in your living room, it's a mistake to ignore it.

Q. It's a mistake not to get the rugs cleaned, too.

A. A big mistake.

Q. How do you handle celebrities who misbehave in public?

A. Hey, that's a trade secret, but when you're dealing with people who have a low Social I.Q., let's say it's best to try to redirect their behavior as you would a child who acts out. Keep in mind, though, that celebrities are subject to the same rules as everyone else, but when they make a mistake, it's in the newspaper and on TV. Reminding them of that component usually helps.

Q. What do you think are the most important rules of Social I.Q.?

A. Well, there are the Ten Commandments of Social I.Q. as we documented earlier, but the most important rules are the most basic ones: Treat people as you would like to be treated in their situation; always return phone calls; never show up late; send thank you notes. You can add any ones you've read (or invented yourself) that are the most important to you.

Everyone has his or her own personal pet peeves, and no matter how trivial they might sound to someone else, to you they're tremendously important. So if it's important to you, it's important.

Q. Is it really so bad to call instead of sending a thank you note?

A. Well, no. It depends on your definition of "really so bad." Picking up a phone and calling instead of taking the time to write your feelings down in your own handwriting is the equivalent of buying someone a fast-food burger instead of cooking a fine meal. They're both food, but one shows that you care a considerable amount more than the other. If that's not "really so bad" to you, then I guess not. To me, a thank you note is absolutely essential.

Q. What things do people do that you find offensive, and how do you react?

A. Reaction is a tricky concept, because you want to let people know that you find their behavior objectionable, but you don't want to behave objectionably yourself. So if someone doesn't return my phone call, is late for a lunch, or doesn't RSVP for an event I'm hosting—three things that I find profoundly rude, I have a choice: I can create a huge scene and tell them that I think they're inconsiderate and thoughtless, or ignore the offensive behavior and therefore expect it to happen again. My third option, the one that I like to employ and find most effective, is to use the Tiffany Theory—tell them that I know they didn't want to offend me but they did anyway, and, in the most complimentary terms I can manage, I explain what the offense was. I often find that it doesn't happen again, and I haven't alienated someone I may want to talk to again.

Q. I'm not letting you off that easy.

A. I never expected you to. Go ahead.

Q. It can sometimes sound like small and large offenses are equal in Social I.Q. Isn't there a pecking order? Aren't some things more important than others?

A. Of course. Now, one thing that really annoys me is when I lend someone a book and they don't return it promptly.

Now I understand why the library charges you for being late. But is that as important as a major family issue? Of course it's not.

Q. Give us an example of a major family issue.

A. All right, let's examine something that's seriously wrong. Let's say two people marry and they both have children from previous relationships. In some cases, you'll see the family—grandparents, even the parents themselves—favoring one set of children over the other. For example, if the man doesn't have custody of the children from his first marriage, but the woman's children are living with the newlywed couple, often her children—who live in the house with them—are favored. This can manifest itself in anything from more pictures of them around the house to better gifts. It's disgusting to do anything but treat the children equally. That is absolutely, profoundly wrong. Children must all be made to feel loved and important. Is that more important than returning a book a week late? You bet it is!

Q. Isn't it hard not to become angry when someone offends you?

A. Of course it is. Sometimes it borders on the impossible. You can get boiling angry at someone who cuts you off on the freeway, but if you examine that angry impulse, you may find that it stems more from the lousy business meeting you just had or the bad news you got yesterday than from the incident on the freeway. Control comes from understanding. If you understand why you feel the way you do, you can control it.

Q. What do you hope to accomplish with this book?

A. Okay, here comes an answer that sounds overblown: I hope to make a better world. If the people who read this book really connect with the ideas in it and put them to use, they will create the ripple effect I've discussed, and help the people around them to be more considerate of others. If that grows from the people who read and believe in this book, I truly believe the world can be a degree more civil—maybe a small degree, but a degree—and in my opinion, that will be a better world. Writing a book is like putting a message in a bottle—you never know who's going to see it or how they might react. My hope is that people will react by examining their feelings and deciding to place more importance on their behavior toward others.

Q. Why are people less interested in manners than they used to be?

A. They're not. People think they're less interested in manners because they don't really understand what manners, or etiquette, means. They think it means placing the spoon and the salad fork in their proper positions. That is an element of manners, but in reality, manners is a set of guidelines for living that can make everyone's life happier, whether it's throwing a formal dinner party or simply walking down the street on the way to the bank. People worry too much about the words *manners* and *etiquette,* and think they refer back to some antiquated code of rigid behavior. In fact, they are very modern concepts when adapted properly. That's why I call my system Social I.Q. instead, so people won't get so hung up on words.

Q. Okay, last question: What was your most awkward situation, and how did you handle it?

A. You mean besides interviewing myself? I can think of hundreds, as anyone can. But since I consider that a personal question, I won't answer it directly. Let me just say that if a situation is properly handled, it won't be awkward at all, because you will have done everything you can *before* the situation turns awkward. So having handled that situation, I think we're ready to move on to what will hopefully be easy and enjoyable for the reader—the Advanced Social I.Q. Test.

Q. Thanks. You've been a great guest.

A. Well, a good interviewer makes a great guest.

THE ADVANCED SOCIAL I.Q. TEST

Suffering is not good for the soul, unless it teaches you to stop suffering.

—Jane Roberts

We don't really have to repeat these directions, do we? Okay, five points for each correct answer.

1. A business phone call should be answered:
   a. within an hour.
   b. the same day.
   c. the same week.
   d. whenever possible.

Answer: B. Started you off with an easy one.

2. You must show up for a business appointment or meal:
   a. on time.
   b. early.
   c. within twenty minutes of the agreed-upon time.
   d. none of the above

Answer: A. Another easy one. Being late is unconscionably rude; being early is unnecessary. Show up on time. All the time.

3. The Ambassador Theory teaches:
   a. how to find a good hotel in Chicago.
   b. how to get people to treat you well.
   c. how to represent yourself in dealings with others.
   d. how to avoid parking tickets.

Answer: C. Remember, you're an ambassador whether you choose to be or not, because people will perceive you that way. Keep that thought in mind, and you'll always be on your best behavior until your best behavior is just your behavior.

4. The Tiffany Theory is a way to:
    a. become a pop star at fifteen.
    b. explain yourself to people.
    c. raise money.
    d. increase the degree to which your message is accepted and understood.

Answer: D. Criticism is rarely effective because it's not absorbed; people get mad when you tell them they're wrong, and they stop listening. Tell the person something positive first, and you have his attention.

5. Some roles are common to all people, like:
    a. teacher.
    b. healer.
    c. minister.
    d. all of the above

Answer: D. Easy, easy, easy. Teachers instruct, healers help, sometimes by doing nothing but listening; ministers listen and offer advice. Everyone does all these things. It's how you play the roles that counts.

6. You're eating dinner and the phone rings. It is polite to.
    a. interrupt your dinner and go answer the phone, letting the dog get a shot at your Beef Wellington.
    b. let the answering machine handle it, and call back as soon as you're finished eating.
    c. turn the machine's volume down, so you can't hear who's calling.
    d. none of the above

Answer: B. There's nothing rude about screening calls, as long as you call back. The same day.

7. You're on the phone and your call waiting beeps. It is polite to:
   a. ask the person you're speaking with to wait, and find out who's calling.
   b. ignore the beep and go on with your conversation.
   c. hang up and forget the whole thing.
   d. none of the above

Answer: B. Don't give the person you're talking to the message that you're just waiting for someone better to call. Exception to the rule: if you're expecting an important business call.

8. When meeting a client, your chief role is that of:
   a. healer.
   b. teacher.
   c. minister.
   d. ambassador.

Answer: D. You're acting in all your usual ambassador roles and literally as an ambassador for your company. Be as polite as you can.

9. Your boss has asked you for a date. You don't want to go. You say:
   a. "I don't mix business and dating."
   b. "Sounds great."
   c. "I'm sorry, but I'm uncomfortable with that."
   d. "Does this mean we have to have sex?"

Answer: C. Well, you are uncomfortable with it, aren't you? And if your boss insists that it's going to be important to your job, you have a great lawsuit on your hands.

10. When asking someone out on a first date:
   a. always ask about a specific event.
   b. ask only for weekends.
   c. find out if you can split the bill.
   d. all of the above

Answer: A. Asking "Are you available Friday?" is unfair. Ask for a specific event—dinner, the theatre, a movie, whatever—and give the other person a fair idea of what's being asked.

11. The check for the first date is paid by:
   a. whomever has the most money.
   b. the man.
   c. the person who did the inviting.
   d. the woman.

Answer: C. Unless there's a prior agreement to split the bill, the person who does the asking does the paying. After the first date, the couple can make their own rules.

12. Men don't like women to call and ask them out. True or false?

Answer: False.

13. The following is *not* one of the Ten Commandments of Social I.Q.:
   a. Thou shalt RSVP to all invitations before the specified date.
   b. Thou shalt bring a small gift when visiting someone's home.
   c. Thou shalt make eye contact.
   d. Thou shalt not tuck thy napkin in thy pants.

Answer: D. Nobody cares about your napkin. But answering invitations promptly, bringing a token to a host or making eye contact during a conversation are essential.

14. You're dating a woman for six weeks and haven't slept with her yet. You should:
   a. use the Tiffany Theory.
   b. tell her it's sex or the door.
   c. use your healer role.
   d. none of the above

Answer: A. Keep in mind—this is not a method to get someone to sleep with you. It is a method to find out what she's thinking. If you present the problem in complimentary terms, you're more likely to get an honest answer without offending someone you care about.

15. The last man you dated was interested solely in sex. The new man you're dating wants to know when you can sleep together. You should:
    a. explain why you're reluctant.
    b. assume you've struck another loser, and bail.
    c. give in and sleep with him.
    d. none of the above

Answer: A. Information is power. If the man knows why you're reluctant, he can react honestly. You'll have a better idea of what kind of man you're dating when he knows the truth.

16. Your six-year-old wants to meet the man you've dated twice. You:
    a. introduce them.
    b. tell the man.
    c. tell the boy you're not ready to introduce them yet.
    d. none of the above

Answer: C. Children form attachments to people very quickly. You don't want to introduce your child until you're sure this man is going to be in your life for a long time.

17. After a couple sleeps together for the first time, the man should:
    a. send a thank you note.
    b. call first thing in the morning.
    c. send flowers.
    d. all or any of the above

Answer: D. "All" is better than "any." Reassurance and courtesy are called for.

18. Thanksgiving's coming up and you're feuding with your brother. What do you do?
   a. Make plans to vacation in Paris.
   b. Call your brother and try to smooth things over for one day.
   c. Call your mother and explain why you can't come.
   d. Go, but avoid your brother at all costs.

Answer: B. Family feuds are inevitable, but can be contained for the sake of all concerned. Try to keep things on an even keel by meeting before Thanksgiving and at least agreeing to be civil.

19. Your sister has told you she's gay. Your best reaction is:
   a. an honest one, no matter what.
   b. acceptance, no matter what.
   c. rejection, no matter what.
   d. none of the above

Answer: B. This is a very vulnerable, difficult time for a gay person. The worst thing you can do is show even a little rejection. This is still your sister, and it's the same sister you had before you knew her sexual orientation. Be a grown-up and accept her. No matter what.

20. Your children are acting rudely at your cousin's home. You don't want to make a scene, but you know they'll react badly if you discipline them now. You:
   a. leave.
   b. discipline them, and make a scene.
   c. ignore it.
   d. none of the above

Answer: D. The best thing to do is isolate the child and explain why this is not acceptable behavior. If the child can't behave, you may have to resort to A.

21. Your old friends don't like your new friends. You:
   a. insist on bringing the new friends along, hoping the two groups will mesh.

    b. use the Tiffany Theory on your old friends.
    c. be an ambassador.
    d. maintain both friendships separately.

Answer: D. You can't force people to like each other. You also don't want to lose your friends, old or new. Just don't bring them together when it's not necessary.

22. Your sister has lost her husband. Your first words:
    a. "I'm so sorry."
    b. "How can I help?"
    c. "You look awful."
    d. "Words can't convey my sorrow."

Answer: B. Your feelings are not as important as your sister's. Deal with them first, and give her all the help you can.

23. When entering an online chat room, the following is called shouting:
    a. changing the topic.
    b. using all capital letters.
    c. writing in vertical lines.
    d. criticizing other people's messages.

Answer: B. It's considered very rude. Don't do it.

24. Invitations for a dinner party should be send out:
    a. a week before the party.
    b. two to three weeks before the party.
    c. a month before the party.
    d. two months before the party.

Answer: B. Two to three weeks is plenty of time to respond, without being so far in advance that nobody remembers the party when it's time to come.

25. Which of the following statements is true
    a. Silence is agreement.
    b. Technology is the enemy of reverence.

c. We are all healers, teachers, and ministers.
d. You have now completed the quiz.
e. all of the above

Answer: E. If you don't remember what any of these means, check pages 219, 37, and 23. And you have now completed the quiz.

Score

10–25: Go back right now and read the whole book again. I've failed.

30–50: You are only retaining one-fourth of what you read. Seek out Evelyn Wood.

55–75: Maybe you should turn the TV off while you're reading.

80–100: You are cleared to go out and mingle with other humans, but keep this book handy as a reference.

105–125: Congratulations! You're an expert on Social I.Q.!

CONCLUSION

I have a simple philosophy. Fill what's empty. Empty what's full. And scratch where it itches.

—ALICE ROOSEVELT LONGWORTH

So, that's it. The Social I.Q. system in a remarkably long nutshell. Used properly, this system should help you in literally every aspect of your life, from talking to the newspaper vendor to asking your true love to marry you. Keep practicing the system, and it will serve you well. But remember, you have to keep vigilant. Like any other muscle, your Social I.Q. will atrophy if you don't exercise it regularly. But the great thing about manners is that the more you use them, the easier they are to use.

Do use your manners. They are all that stands between a civil, considerate world and, alas, the one we have now. You, as an ambassador of Social I.Q., can go out into the world and change that. Put on your dress uniform, polish up those medals, put your completed Social I.Q. Test in your pocket, and go do battle with the forces of rudeness and thoughtlessness! You are armed to the teeth with your knowledge, and your practice will make you stronger.

I'm glad you recognized that the subject of manners is important. You have demonstrated that by buying and reading this book. Now, with the knowledge you've gained, you can put the Social I.Q. system into practice in your daily life. Send out ripples. Make the world a better place.

I sincerely hope that I run into you on the street very soon. I'll know you by your friendly smile and polite manner. And I will be very proud.

Templates for Letters, Notes, and Invitations

LETTERS AND NOTES

Thank You Note

Rules: Always mention the gift specifically. Mention the occasion for which the gift was given. Even if you don't like the gift, don't lie, but be diplomatic. No typing.

For a gift you like:

Dear Mom,

Thank you so much for the lovely fruit bowl. I've already set it on Grandma's antique table, and it brightens up the whole room. I love the bowl, but the fact that you were thinking of Alan and me on our anniversary is the real gift. Thanks again. I'll be talking to you soon.

Love,
Jenny

See? Not so hard.
For a gift you *don't* like:

Dear Mom,

Thank you very much for remembering our anniversary. The fruit bowl is just the kind of thing that makes a room complete, and Alan and I both appreciate your thoughts of us on our special day. We hope to see you very soon.

Love,
Jenny

A Note of Condolence

Rules: Concentrate on *their* loss, not yours. Try to remember a positive anecdote. Refrain from the phrase, "Words can't express my sorrow...", and absolutely, write the note in your own handwriting.

Dear Cousin Ralph,

My thoughts are with you following the loss of your father. I will always remember him as a kind and humorous man, and cherish the memory of the fishing trips he took me on when I was little. Please don't hesitate to let me know if there's anything I can do for you.

Love,
Marjorie

Acknowledgment of a Condolence Note

Rules: No preprinted cards from the funeral home. No store-bought cards. No typing.

Dear Marjorie,

Thank you for your kind words of condolence. Your memories of my father were very sweet, and help to comfort us in this very difficult time.

Love,
Ralph

After-Dinner Notes

Purpose: Acknowledging the hospitality of someone who invited you to dinner. Can also be used as a post–first-date note.

Rules: Be cordial, write in longhand (no typing), and send promptly.

Dear Wanda,

Bob and I had a marvelous time at your house last night. The dinner was delicious and the conversation was just as satisfying. We'll be calling to invite you over very soon. Thanks for inviting us.

Sincerely,
Pat

Letter of Recommendation

Purpose: To recommend a former employee when he or she is searching for a new job.

Rules: Be honest, be fair, and don't let emotions get in the way of the facts. This absolutely, *must* be type-written (yes, a computer printer is fine), and written in the form of a business letter. If you have been contacted by a specific company interested in your former employee, address the letter to the person making the inquiry. If it is a general letter the employee has requested upon termination, layoff, or resignation, address the letter "To Whom It May Concern."

April 22, 1999

To Whom It May Concern:

Mr. F Friday has been my faithful employee for seventeen years. During that time, he has proven himself resourceful, trustworthy, able, intelligent, and helpful. My professional circumstances have recently changed, and I no longer have need of his services, and have regretfully parted company with Mr. Friday. I have never had any serious complaint about his work, and recommend him wholeheartedly.

Please feel free to contact me with any questions you might have regarding Mr. Friday, whom I sincerely hope will be an employee of yours very soon.

Sincerely,
R. Crusoe

Note: If the employee has been discharged for cause or due to some inadequacy in performance, but you are still inclined to recommend him, the rules are almost the same. Don't let negative emotions cloud the issue, but don't lie. Present the facts in a positive light. A sample follows.

April 22, 1999

To Whom It May Concern:

Mr. Igor Henchman has been in my employ for the past six months. During that time, he performed the tasks that were required of him without complaint, and was always prompt. I am unable to employ Mr. Henchman any longer.

If you have any questions, please send them to me and I will try to answer them to the best of my ability.

Sincerely,
Dr. Victor Frankenstein, M.D.

Letter of Complaint

Purpose: To bring to the attention of a company official some inadequacy regarding either the company's product or an employee of the company, and to ask for retribution.

Rules: Always typed. Send it to the highest-ranking official in the company whose name you can find. Be to-the-point and don't rant. Tell them what you want. Keep it short, one page if possible.

April 22, 1999

Mr. H. Helmsley
President
Empire State Building
W. 34th Street
New York, NY 10036

Dear Mr. Helmsley:

On visiting your property, the Empire State Building,
yesterday, I encountered a situation which I believe
warrants your close attention. I am appalled at the lack
of security in your building and think you should take
immediate steps.

After a rather harrowing day in Manhattan, I was
visiting the observation tower of your building when an
oversized ape pulled me from the safety of the tower and
held me over the harrowing drop to the pavement for
some minutes. It wasn't until city officials were
notified, and airplanes sent by the city managed to
contain the beast, that I was safely returned to the tower.

Frankly, I believe this incident demonstrates a serious
lack of security measures on your part. Until sufficient
barriers are placed on the observation tower, and a
private security force armed with ape-tranquilizing darts
is in place, I will refrain from visiting a Helmsley
property again.

I believe that a very sincere apology is needed as well. I
hope to hear from you very soon with the news that the
steps I have outlined have been taken.

Sincerely,
Ms. F. Wray

INVITATIONS

Wedding Invitations

Formal invitation:

Mr. and Mrs. Harrison Beauty
request the honor of your presence
at the marriage of their daughter
Sleeping
to
Mr. Prince Joshua Charming
on Sunday, the twenty-sixth of April
One thousand, nine hundred and ninety-nine
at three o'clock
Unitarian Church
Morristown, New Jersey

Reception card: Sent with the invitation to those invited to the reception. Usually printed on cover stock.

Reception immediately following the ceremony
The Manor
642 Pleasant Valley Road
West Orange, New Jersey
The favor of a reply is requested
1918 Morris Avenue, Morristown, New Jersey 07846

Notes: It is acceptable to include the groom's parents in the invitation as well. The reception card is usually sent with an envelope, addressed to the RSVP address, and stamped before sending. This makes it convenient for the recipient of the invitation to RSVP promptly.

Wedding Announcement

Purpose: To announce the marriage to those who have not been invited to the wedding.

Mr. and Mrs. Harrison Beauty
and
Dr. and Mrs. Arnold Charming
announce the marriage of their children
Sleeping Beauty
and
Mr. Prince Joshua Charming
on Sunday, April 26
one thousand, nine hundred and ninety-nine
Morristown, New Jersey

Shower Invitation

Purpose: To invite people to either wedding or baby showers.
Rules: Less formal, but include all the information, and make sure there's an RSVP address or phone number, or both.

You're invited to Rosemary Woodhouse's baby shower!
on Sunday, October 31 at 3 P.M.
at the apartment of Minnie and Roman Castavet
345 West 59th Street, Manhattan, Apt. 666
RSVP Minnie Castavet (212) 555-5559

Birth Announcement

Note: Usually presented with the name of the baby and the date of birth on the outside fold, and the announcement on the inside.

On the Outside:

> *Damien Lucifer Woodhouse*
> *October 31, 1999*

On the Inside:

> *Rosemary and Guy Woodhouse*
> *announce the birth of their son,*
> *Damien Lucifer*
> *on October 31, 1999*
> *Weight: Six pounds, six ounces*
> *Length: Twenty-one inches*
>
> *Mr. and Mrs. Guy Woodhouse*
> *345 West 57th Street*
> *New York, NY 10666*

Adoption Announcement

> *Mr. and Mrs. George Kent*
> *are pleased to announce the adoption of*
> *Clark Jorel*
> *Age: Six months*

A Note From the Author

As social mores change (and they do constantly), I have every intention of revising and updating *Raising Your Social I.Q.* I'd appreciate your feedback, and would love to hear your stories of awkward situations, and how you handled them.

Please feel free to contact me at:

Michael Levine
Social I.Q.
5750 Wilshire Boulevard
Suite 555
Los Angeles, CA 90036

Or (and in this case it's perfectly appropriate) by E-mail at:

levinepr@earthlink.net

Thanks for reading this book. I hope it enriches your life and the lives of those you love.

Called by *USA Today* "one of Hollywood's smartest and most respected executives," Michael Levine, forty-four, heads the Levine Communications Office in Los Angeles. He is the author of nine other books. His articles have appeared in the *Los Angeles Times, Wall Street Journal, Reader's Digest,* and *USA Today,* among others.